NAMING GOD

CHRISTIAN AND MUSLIM PERSPECTIVES

Previously Published Records of Building Bridges Seminars

The Road Ahead: A Christian–Muslim Dialogue, Michael Ipgrave, editor (London: Church House, 2002)

Scriptures in Dialogue: Christians and Muslims Studying the Bible and the Qur'ān Together, Michael Ipgrave, editor (London: Church House, 2004)

Bearing the Word: Prophecy in Biblical and Qur'ānic Perspective, Michael Ipgrave, editor (London: Church House, 2005)

Building a Better Bridge: Muslims, Christians, and the Common Good, Michael Ipgrave, editor (Washington, DC: Georgetown University Press, 2008)

Justice and Rights: Christian and Muslim Perspectives, Michael Ipgrave, editor (Washington, DC: Georgetown University Press, 2009)

Humanity: Texts and Contexts: Christian and Muslim Perspectives, Michael Ipgrave and David Marshall, editors (Washington, DC: Georgetown University Press, 2011)

Communicating the Word: Revelation, Translation, and Interpretation in Christianity and Islam, David Marshall, editor (Washington, DC: Georgetown University Press, 2011)

Science and Religion: Christian and Muslim Perspectives, David Marshall, editor (Washington, DC: Georgetown University Press, 2012)

Tradition and Modernity: Christian and Muslim Perspectives, David Marshall, editor (Washington, DC: Georgetown University Press, 2012)

Prayer: Christian and Muslim Perspectives, David Marshall and Lucinda Mosher, editors (Washington, DC: Georgetown University Press, 2013)

Death, Resurrection, and Human Destiny: Christian and Muslim Perspectives, David Marshall and Lucinda Mosher, editors (Washington, DC: Georgetown University Press, 2014)

The Community of Believers: Christian and Muslim Perspectives, Lucinda Mosher and David Marshall, editors (Washington, DC: Georgetown University Press, 2015)

Sin, Forgiveness, and Reconciliation: Christian and Muslim Perspectives, Lucinda Mosher and David Marshall, editors (Washington, DC: Georgetown University Press, 2016)

God's Creativity and Human Action: Christian and Muslim Perspectives, Lucinda Mosher and David Marshall, editors (Washington, DC: Georgetown University Press, 2017)

Monotheism and Its Complexities: Christian and Muslim Perspectives, Lucinda Mosher and David Marshall, editors (Washington, DC: Georgetown University Press, 2018)

Power—Divine and Human: Christian and Muslim Perspectives, Lucinda Mosher and David Marshall, editors (Washington, DC: Georgetown University Press, 2019)

A World of Inequalities: Christian and Muslim Perspectives, Lucinda Mosher, editor (Washington, DC: Georgetown University Press, 2021)

Freedom: Christian and Muslim Perspectives, Lucinda Mosher, editor (Washington, DC: Georgetown University Press, 2021)

NAMING GOD

CHRISTIAN AND MUSLIM PERSPECTIVES

A Record of the Nineteenth Building Bridges Seminar

Hosted online by
Georgetown University
June 7–11, 2021

Lucinda Mosher, Editor

Georgetown University Press / Washington, DC

Library of Congress Cataloging-in-Publication Data

Names: Building Bridges Seminar (19th : 2021), author. | Mosher, Lucinda, editor.
Title: Naming God : Christian and Muslim perspectives / editor, Lucinda Mosher.
Description: Washington, DC : Georgetown University Press, 2023. | Includes index.
Identifiers: LCCN 2022044868 (print) | LCCN 2022044869 (ebook) |
ISBN 9781647123666 (paperback) | ISBN 9781647123659 (hardcover) |
ISBN 9781647123673 (ebook)
Subjects: LCSH: God (Christianity)—Name—Congresses. | God (Islam)—Name—Congresses.
Classification: LCC BT180.N2 B79 2021 (print) | LCC BT180.N2 (ebook) |
DDC 231—dc23/eng/20230605
LC record available at https://lccn.loc.gov/2022044868
LC ebook record available at https://lccn.loc.gov/2022044869

24 23 9 8 7 6 5 4 3 2 First printing
Printed in the United States of America

Cover design by Nathan Putens
Interior design by Paul Hotvedt

Contents

Part Three: Naming God in Devotional Practice

Part Four: Reflection

Participants in the Building Bridges Seminar 2021

Hussein Abdulsater, University of Notre Dame, USA
Muhammad Modassir Ali, Hamad Bin Khalifa University, Qatar
Ahmet Alibašić, University of Sarajevo, Bosnia and Herzegovina
Mehdi Azaiez, Université catholique de Louvain, Belgium; University of Lorraine, France
John Azumah, The Sanneh Institute, Ghana
Jonathan Brown, Georgetown University, USA
Yousef Casewit, University of Chicago, USA
Emmanuel Clapsis, Hellenic College and Holy Cross Greek Orthodox School of Theology, USA
Maria Massi Dakake, George Mason University, USA
Susan Eastman, Duke University Divinity School, USA
Lucy Gardner, St. Stephen's House, Oxford, UK
Christopher M. Hays, Biblical Seminary of Colombia, Colombia
Damian Howard, SJ, Jesuit British Province, UK
Tuba Işık, Humboldt University of Berlin, Germany
Veli-Matti Kärkkäinen, Fuller Theological Seminary, USA
Daniel Madigan, SJ, Georgetown University, USA
David Marshall, World Council of Churches, Switzerland
Mahan Mirza, University of Notre Dame, USA
Esther Mombo, St Paul's University, Limuru, Kenya
Lucinda Mosher, Hartford International University for Religion and Peace, USA
Kenan Musić, University of Sarajevo, Bosnia and Herzegovina
Martin Nguyen, Fairfield University, USA
Elizabeth Phillips, University of Cambridge; Durham University, UK
Christoph Schwöbel, University of St. Andrews, UK
Reza Shah-Kazemi, Aga Khan Centre, UK
Muna Tatari, University of Paderborn, Germany
Staff: Samuel Wagner, Georgetown University, USA

Introduction

In one sense, Muslims and Christians agree that God is unnamable. So asserted moderator Dan Madigan as he introduced the topic on which the nineteenth convening of the Building Bridges Seminar would focus. That is, he clarified, both traditions affirm that "God is not just one of the things-in-the-world that can be named and so identified and defined." In another sense, however, Muslims and Christians would agree that God has many names. These are *not* names that humans invent for God, he explained. Rather,

> they are names that God reveals to humanity; names by which human beings are to call upon God; names that reveal not so much *what* God is, but *who* God is, and more to the point who God is *in relation to us*. God cannot be constrained or contained by the names, but God can be praised by them, can be called upon in supplication, can be remembered by them for the wonderful works God has done and continues to do. Repeating the names, praying them, praising by means of them leads us more deeply into the life of faith, even to the point of being re-made, as it were, in the image of God. Clearly, each of our traditions would understand this way of expressing things in its own way, but we can recognize a certain commonality that makes our dialogue possible.[1]

This is the shared, sensitive, and sometimes contentious environment into which Christians and Muslims venture when they speak to one another about the proper naming of God. After three years of wrestling with public themes (divine and human power; inequality of several sorts; divine and human freedom), the Building Bridges Seminar was ready to turn its attention to such questions.

Believed to be the longest-running international dialogue of Christian and Muslim scholars, the Building Bridges Seminar was initiated in 2002 by then–Archbishop of Canterbury George Carey. Rowan Williams sustained the dialogue during the ten years of his tenure in that office. Since 2012 it has been stewarded by Georgetown University. The Building Bridges Seminar's practice is to invite selected Christian and Muslim scholar-believers into a conversation circle for the purpose of dialogical close reading of texts (scriptural and otherwise) over several days.

At Building Bridges Seminar convenings—which have been held in the United Kingdom, the United States, Qatar, Bosnia and Herzegovina, Turkey, Italy, Singapore, and Switzerland—Christian and Muslim participants are always nearly equal in number. A significant number of each are women. Most of the Christians are Anglican or Roman Catholic, but some have been Orthodox, Lutheran, Methodist, Pentecostal, or Presbyterian. Most Muslims are Sunni, but Shiʿa have always taken part. The collection of texts that participants are expected to read, analyze, and comment upon are chosen and organized to prompt deep discussion of a carefully framed, multilayered theme such as prophethood, prayer, revelation, human destiny, community, or forgiveness.

Plans for a June 2020 convening in Tübingen, Germany, were upended by the rapid global spread of the novel coronavirus. In 2021, rather than postpone again, the Seminar determined to meet online. The topic chosen for 2020, *Naming God*, was retained. The agenda featured three themes: the naming of God in Christian and Muslim scriptures; reflection on the nature of these names in Christian and Muslim foundational philosophical and theological traditions; and Christian and Muslim practices of calling on God by God's names in communal and private prayer. Some might say that this last theme is the most significant of the three since, as Dan Madigan explained,

> only prayer can lead us more deeply into the reality of God. However, it also ties us into our scriptures and into the history of interpretation and reception of those texts. Our calling on God's Name both grows out of scripture and constantly leads us back there. It binds us into a community of faith that spans the centuries.

The approach taken by the Seminar to consideration of Christian and Muslim perspectives on "naming God" was consonant with strategies employed in its earlier study of "monotheism and its complexities."[2] That is, the planners (while acknowledging that engagement of Christians and Muslims with one another on the topic of God per se has always been direct and forceful) endeavored to avoid making the traditionally contested doctrine of the Trinity the conversation's starting point. They preferred instead to begin from the concern in both traditions, each in its own way, to affirm God's uniqueness. Thus, the primacy remains with the God who reveals Godself rather than with a concept of a unity that is, as it were, the thing that qualifies God to be God.

Whatever the topic it takes on, the Building Bridges Seminar strives always to help participants gain better understanding of each other's tradition, to wrestle with theological complexities, and to improve the quality of their disagreements. Its structure facilitates this by conducting almost all of its work in closed session; by organizing the participants into small discussion groups that remain constant throughout a convening; and by opening and closing each day with a robust plenary conversation. This last element was missing in 2021. Meeting virtually across many time zones precluded systematic scheduling of daily plenaries. Often a convening of the Building Bridges Seminar includes a public session featuring overview lectures. In 2021 planners opted for the simplicity and informality of closed sessions. On day 1 of the 2021 Building Bridges Seminar, participants heard six lectures, each introducing a set of texts to be studied on one of the days to come.

When asked to assess the experience of a virtual convening, one scholar noted that it had certain advantages: "no one had to get a visa or cross a border." Another, however, lamented its lack of opportunity for experts to sit together and talk informally. "Those soft instructional experiences happen," she quipped, "only when we're trapped together in a retreat center!" Even so, another participant was quick to acknowledge that the online conversation had worked better than she had anticipated—perhaps even as well as would have been the case had the seminar met in-person. In part, this was the result of beginning from a point of familiarity: everyone involved had participated in at least one previous seminar. "We were right to not invite new persons this time," she said.

Indeed, the online small groups were a lot like the "in-person" small groups of previous years. Each had its own style, its own variation on the Seminar's method. What was consistent from one group to the next was palpable closeness among the members of each of those virtual study circles. While preference for meeting face-to-face was nearly universal, there was also consensus that—in spite of almost overwhelming time-zone challenges—it is possible for the Building Bridges Seminar to convene in cyberspace in a manner marked by collegiality and considerable depth.

To encourage further study and dialogue, each lecture from the 2021 convening is presented in this volume as an essay, followed immediately by the set of study texts it introduces. Hence, each of the three parts that make up the bulk of this book includes four chapters. In part 1, Naming God in Scripture, "Walking the Knife-Edge: Christian Scripture on Labeling the Ineffable" by Christopher M. Hays, is followed by "Bible Passages on Naming God," which offers selections from each testament. "Calling God by His Names: The Subject and Object of 'Naming God,'" by Maria Massi Dakake, is followed by "Qur'an and Hadiths on Naming God: Selections for Dialogue." This chapter provides eighteen passages from fifteen suras grouped under three headings: God's "Most Beautiful" Names; false gods as "names that you have named"; and devotional/ritual invocations of God's Name. Six hadiths are also included—among them, a list of the ninety-nine Beautiful Names.

Part 2, Naming God in Theological Discourse, opens with "What's in a Name? A Christian Historical Perspective on Naming God" by Christoph Schwöbel. "Christian Theological Discourse on Naming God: Selections for Dialogue" provides excerpts from the writings of Pseudo-Dionysius the Areopagite, John of Damascus, Thomas Aquinas, Meister Eckhart, and Martin Luther, plus a portion of the Westminster Confession of Faith (1646). "Commentaries on the Divine Names: Two Exemplars from the Islamic Tradition," by Yousef Casewit, is followed by "Muslim Theological Discourse on Naming God: Selections for Dialogue"—excerpts from the writings of al-Juwaynī, al-Ghazālī, and al-Tilimsānī.

In part 3, Naming God in Devotional Practice, Lucy Gardner's essay, "Naming God in Christian Prayer and Worship: Its Impact on Spiritual Formation," is followed by "Christian Devotional Literature on Naming God: Selections for Dialogue"—texts of various hymns. "A Matter of Theurgy: The Impact of Naming God in Muslim Devotional Practice," by Reza Shah-Kazemi, is followed by "Muslim Devotional Literature on Naming God: Selections for Dialogue," offering excerpts from the writings of Ibn 'Aṭā'illah and Rumi, plus two litanies. Part 4, Reflection, provides "Conversations in Cyberspace" by Lucinda Mosher—an overview of themes discussed and a sampler of interactions among the 2021 seminar participants.

Throughout this volume, diacritics are employed sparingly. Dates are "CE" unless otherwise indicated. We are grateful to many publishers for permission to use the material excerpted in this volume. All are credited as they occur. Unless otherwise noted, Qur'an quotations are according to *The Study Quran*, edited by S. H. Nasr, et al. (HarperOne, 2015); used by permission).[3] Unless otherwise noted, Bible passages are according to the New Revised Standard Version of the Bible, copyright 1989 by the Division of Christian Education of the National Council of the Churches of Christ in the USA (used by permission; all rights reserved). We are especially grateful to Professor Hossein Kamaly (Hartford International University for Religion and Peace) and Dr. Rasoul Naghavi Nia (Mufid Academic Seminary) for their help with the translation and transliteration of one of the examples of Muslim devotional literature included in part 3.

Deep appreciation goes to Georgetown University president John J. DeGioia for his ongoing support of the Building Bridges Seminar. As in previous years, David Marshall (the project's academic director) and Daniel Madigan (its chair) were instrumental in setting the 2021 theme, organizing the roster of scholars, and—in careful conversation with those designated as presenters—choosing the texts to be studied. Two others also played strategic roles in the 2021 gathering: Lucinda Mosher (Hartford International University), the Seminar's rapporteur; and Samuel Wagner, who, as Georgetown University's director of dialogue and Catholic identity, serves as the Seminar's coordinator, working closely with the chair and academic director in planning the annual meeting. Finally, gratitude is extended to Georgetown University's Berkley Center for Religion, Peace, and World Affairs, which provides an ongoing base of operations and online presence for the Seminar and has made the publication of this book possible; and to Al Bertrand and the staff of Georgetown University Press for their patient assistance.

Notes

1. From Daniel Madigan's "concept note" to the Building Bridges Seminar staff and planning team, January 30, 2020.

2. For the 2016 proceedings, see Lucinda Mosher and David Marshall, eds., *Monotheism and Its Complexities: Christian and Muslim Perspectives* (Washington, DC: Georgetown University Press, 2018).

3. Quran verses: 1:17; 2:31–33; 6:118–121; 7:70–72, 114–115, 180, 255; 12: 39–40; 17: 107–110; 22:58–65, 34–35, 39–41; 24:35–38; 25:58–63; 40: 1–3; 53:19–23; 59:22–34; 87:1, 14–15 from *The Study Quran* by Seyyed Hossein Nasr, Editor-in-Chief, Caner K. Dagli, Maria Massi Dakake, Joseph E.B. Lumbard, Mohammed Rustom. Copyright 2015 by Seyyed Hossein Nasr. Used by permission of HarperCollins Publishers.

Part One

Naming God in Scripture

1

Walking the Knife-Edge

Christian Scripture on Labeling the Ineffable

Christopher M. Hays

Contemplating God is dangerous business. The Babylonian Talmud (Hagigah 14b) tells of four men—Simeon ben ʿAzzai, Simeon ben Zoma, Rabbi Elisha ben Abuyah, and Rabbi Akiba ben Yosef—who had visions of heaven. Ben ʿAzzai cast a look at the divine realm and died forthwith. Ben Zoma went mad at the sight. The heavenly revelations made Elisha ben Abuyah into a heretic. Later rabbis refused to use his name; they called him simply Aher (The Other Guy). Only Akiba emerged unscathed from his mystical ascent: orthodox, sane, and alive.

Similarly, when someone names God—attempting thereby to define some aspect of God—they walk a knife-edge between the venerable Rabbi Akiba and the heretic Aher. After all, naming God entails labeling the ineffable. And yet the Bible itself oscillates between denying that God can be seen and describing how God shows Godself anyway. In this chapter I outline how Old Testament texts name God, their authors sometimes drawing on the names of Canaanite gods, in conjunction with their own experience with the divine. Thereafter I turn to the Greek New Testament, exploring how Christians, in response to their experience of the divine in Jesus, continued that process of naming God in ways that, in the eyes of many Jews, made them no better than Aher the heretic. But if one is to trust the truthfulness of the Scripture, these audacious ventures to name God were ultimately revelatory, even if being hardly exhaustive of who God is. This chapter describes how the biblical authors dared to apply names to God in ways that drew on their ancestral tradition and yet sometimes threatened to violate that tradition as they responded to the theological insights of their pagan neighbors and even to new experiences of the divine.

Naming God in the Jewish Scriptures

The three most common names for God in the Old Testament are Elohim, Adonai, and YHWH (often called "the Tetragrammaton"). Elohim is the standard epithet for the divine in Hebrew, simply translated "G/god" and capable of denoting Israel's deity or "gods" more generally (e.g., Ex. 12:12; Josh. 24:15).[1] Another common name for Israel's God is Adonai; it is aptly translated "L/lord," and, as with the English term *lord*, Adonai can denote the divine Lord (with a capital L), as in Isaiah 6:1 (see also Gen. 15:2; Deut. 3:24; 2 Sam. 7:18–20), or a human master (Gen. 24:14, 27, 35–36).[2] Most importantly, there is the Tetragrammaton, the four-consonant name YHWH, which is also translated "LORD" in English but written with small caps to differentiate it from the translation of Adonai as "Lord."[3] When scholars read out this name, we pronounce it "Yahweh," but one does well to be circumspect in enunciating the name outright because Jewish people have stringently avoided uttering it since well before the time of Christ.[4] Instead of saying "Yahweh," the more generic term *Adonai* was verbalized.[5] Eventually, to remind oral readers of the Hebrew Bible to do this, the vowels from *Adonai* were written above and below the *YHWH* consonants of the Tetragrammaton, which subsequently led to the practice of translating the divine name as "Jehovah."[6] In any scenario, the Israelite deity's most characteristic and unique name was YHWH, although biblical writers often combine and oscillate between the Tetragrammaton and the more generic Elohim.

YHWH Means Being Israel's Covenant God: Exodus 3

The "origin story" of the Tetragrammaton is found in Exodus 3, when Moses meets the LORD at the burning bush. Moses quickly comes to understand that this Elohim is his ancestral deity, but he has to prod God a bit to disclose their identity specifically as Yahweh. God explains that unique name with the statement "I will be who I will be"—*'ehyeh 'asher 'ehyeh*, or *'ehyeh* for short (Exod. 3:14).

The text explains the name of Yahweh through a sort of popular or punning etymology based on the similarities between *'ehyeh* and Yahweh; the two words look like first- and third-person singular conjugations of the related verbal roots *hayah* and *hawah*, meaning broadly "to be." This popular etymology has, frankly, not aged well—at least if it was intended to provide listeners with clarity—because what *'ehyeh 'asher 'ehyeh* means is hotly contested.[7] The Greek translation of the Hebrew Bible, called the Septuagint (LXX), rendered the phrase as *egō eimi ho ōn*, "I am the one who is"—a rendering that will be important for our interpretation of the Greek New

Testament. That Greek translation, which lies behind the traditional English rendering "I am who I am," emphasizes God's absolute being or transcendent existence in ways that fit with the sort of Greek philosophical interests that predominated at the time the LXX was being translated.

In spite of this tradition, *'ehyeh 'asher 'ehyeh*, composed of two imperfect Hebrew verbs, can be more satisfactorily rendered "I will be who I will be."[8] The text should not be understood as a statement about abstract divine ontology but as an affirmation of the LORD's freedom to act as the LORD will.[9] As the context makes clear (3:7–9, 15–22), this freedom should not be construed in simple libertarian terms; it is a freedom that commits without coercion to being the covenant God of Israel, fulfilling the vows made to Israel's ancestors, delivering the Israelites from slavery, and leading them into the land promised to their forefathers.[10] To be YHWH means to be the God of the Patriarchs, the God of Israel's past, and simultaneously the God who will guide them into the future.

Seeing and Explaining YHWH: Exodus 33–34; Isaiah 6

This interpretation of the name of the LORD in terms of God's unfolding covenant relationship with Israel is made even more explicit as the book of Exodus progresses.[11] Consider the events of Exodus 33–34, which occur right between the golden calf incident (an event of grievous covenant violation; Exod. 32) and the covenant renewal (34:10–28). After Moses pled with God to have mercy on the Israelites, and succeeded (Exod. 33:17), the prophet decided to press his luck, and entreated the LORD, "Show me your glory" (33:18).

This might seem a rather foolhardy thing for Moses to request. As God explains to Moses in verse 20, for a sinful mortal to see God's face will result in death; much the same perspective lies behind Isaiah the prophet's cry of despair (Isa. 6:5) "Woe is me! I am lost, for I am a man of unclean lips . . . ; yet my eyes have seen the King, the LORD of hosts (Yahweh Tzebaoth)."[12] Nonetheless, other passages affirm that Moses *did* speak to God face-to-face, including Exodus 33:11, just seven verses prior to Moses's request![13] These contradictions likely owe to the divergent sources combined in the Torah, but that is not to say that the Torah editors were ignorant of them. Maintaining both ideas—that you cannot see God and that some people do see God—is one canonical way of communicating the paradox of an infinite God who chooses to reveal Godself to unworthy mortals.

Within this particular episode, that same point is made in a slightly different way. Here God denies Moses's request to see the divine glory but concedes to him the revelation of divine *goodness* in combination with the proclamation of God's own name (33:19–20). Perhaps expressing a similar compromise in more physical terms, God says that Moses will be allowed to see not the divine face but the divine back (33:22–23).

God then passes by Moses and declares the name YHWH, the meaning of which is explained as "I will be gracious to whom I will be gracious, and will show mercy on whom I will show mercy."[14] These phraseologies are strikingly similar to the earlier affirmation of divine freedom "I will be who I will be."[15] This interpretation of the name fits with God's promise to reveal the divine goodness to Moses (Exod. 33:19). Thus, the Lord explains that being YHWH consists essentially in choosing to show mercy to whomever they will, particularly the covenant people (who had just committed gross idolatry), without thereby suspending the prerogative to judge and punish as well.[16]

The Naming of Israel's God Outside of Israel: Numbers 24; Genesis 14

Although the biblical authors present the Lord's identity primarily as Israel's covenant God, they also selectively adapted names for God from their Canaanite neighbors. For example, the Old Testament often calls God *'El* or *'El 'Elyon*, the latter of which is translated "God Most High," or as *ho hupsistos* in the LXX.[17] *'El* could be a generic appellative denoting deity, but *'El* was also the name of the high god of the Canaanite pantheon, and *'Elyon* was an associated Canaanite deity.[18] The Old Testament authors, being fully aware of the Canaanite antecedents for this language, worked those names into their descriptions of YHWH, as in the account of Melchizedek in Genesis 14.

Melchizedek was the king-priest of the city of Salem, who blessed Abraham after the patriarch routed the military forces of an enemy king. Melchizedek is called a "priest of 'El 'Elyon" (14:18) and he blesses Abraham in the name of his god, claiming that Abraham was granted victory by 'El 'Elyon, whom Melchizedek describes as the "maker of heaven and earth" (an attribute that Canaanite religion ascribed to 'El).[19] Rather than disputing the pagan priest's theology, Abraham appears to assent to Melchizedek's assertion, only pausing to ascribe to YHWH the name "'El 'Elyon, maker of heaven and earth" (v. 22). In other words, Abraham accepts the veracity of the pagan priest's assertions about 'El 'Elyon and links the Canaanite creator god with his own covenant deity.

Or consider Balaam, a pagan oracle hired by Balak, the king of Moab, to curse the Israelites so that Balak could drive them out of his territory (Num. 22:4–6). Although Balaam accepts the maledictory commission, he finds himself unable to do what he was paid for because when he attempts to jinx

Israel, the spirit of Elohim comes upon him (24:4) and YHWH puts words of blessing in his mouth (22:38; 23:5, 12, 16). Even though Balaam describes himself as "one who hears the words of 'El, and knows the knowledge of 'Elyon, who sees the vision of Shaddai" (Num. 24:15)—using three names for Canaanite deities—the blessing Balaam pronounces derives from the LORD. Thus, Israel's God absorbs the names of Canaanite gods while co-opting their oracle for Israel's blessing.

Allow me to say a bit more about the name *Shaddai*, that third divine epithet invoked by Balaam (Num. 24:15). The etymology of *Shaddai* is contested, but the LXX often translates *Shaddai* as *pantokratōr*, which is why English translations of the name read "God Almighty."[20] At times, this seems apt, as when 'El Shaddai is depicted as a God of war (Ps. 68:14; Isa. 13:6; Ezek. 1:24; Joel 1:15; Job 6:4); in such contexts, *'El Shaddai* is functionally similar to the moniker "Lord of Hosts," *Yahweh Tzebaoth*, that appears in Isaiah 6:5 as well as pervading the former and latter prophets.[21] Both those names exalt God's power as the one who directs the armies of men (1 Sam. 17:45) and of angels (1 Kings 22:19; 2 Kings 21:5).

Nonetheless, there is a strong case to be made that *Shaddai* derives from the word *shad*, which means "breast." *Shad* was an epithet for *Asherah*, a female Canaanite fertility deity who was 'El's consort and was associated with breastfeeding.[22] While the Hebrew Bible does not describe YHWH as a goddess, various texts do associate the LORD with maternal characteristics, indicating that YHWH bears attributes that polytheistic religions associated with female deities.[23]

Accordingly, the LORD is sometimes called Shaddai specifically in the capacity of providing offspring, as in the fertility promises to the patriarchs (Gen. 17:1–6, 28:3, 35:11, 48:3–4).[24] The connection of Shaddai to fertility is most explicit in Jacob's deathbed benediction of Joseph, which invokes Shaddai to bless Joseph with *birkot shadayim*, "blessings of the breasts and of the womb" (Gen. 49:25). By calling the LORD *Shaddai*, the Israelites expressed that YHWH was the source of the fertility blessings, which Canaanites attributed to Asherah. "Orthodox" Yahwists would not go so far as to affirm the existence of Asherah but, having already subsumed pagan conceptions of 'El into their view of the LORD, they also incorporated key virtues of 'El's consort.[25]

Naming God Out of the Experience of God: Genesis 16

One of the most overt examples of Israelites adopting non-Israelite theology appears in Genesis 16, with Hagar. Hagar is an Egyptian slave girl whose mistress, Sarah, gives her to Abraham as a surrogate. When Hagar conceives,

Sarah grows jealous and abuses Hagar, who subsequently flees back toward Egypt. She makes it as far as a spring on the road to Shur, where she encounters the "angel of the LORD" (Gen. 16:9–11), who informs her that God has taken heed of her abuse and will recompense her with a multitude of descendants through the son she carries.[26] She is told to name him Ishmael, which means "God hears." By naming her son in this fashion, the angel tells her how to interpret her experience of being abused by Sarah and blessed by the LORD.

Hagar marvels: "Have I really seen God and remained alive after seeing him?" (Gen. 16:13). At this juncture in the narrative both Hagar and the author claim, staggeringly, that she has seen not just the angel of the LORD but indeed the LORD themselves. This is likely the consequence of redactional layering in the Genesis account. Gerhard von Rad argues that the oldest versions of the tradition narrated a direct encounter between the LORD and Hagar and that the angel of the Lord was later introduced as a mediating figure to soften the notion that Hagar really saw the LORD directly.[27] This reconstruction seems reasonable since this precise interpretive maneuvering can be viewed in LXX translations of some Hebrew texts.[28] But in the canonical form of this passage, the logic of Genesis 16:13 depends on Hagar understanding the angel of the Lord as "a form in which Yahweh appears. . . , God himself in human form."[29]

While it is extraordinary that Hagar saw the LORD and survived, what she does in response to that experience is unparalleled in the Hebrew Bible: she creates a name for God. The name she invents, 'El-Roi, means "The God Who Sees Me."[30] With this name, Hagar underscores that God is a God who sees her and acts on her behalf. God had told her how to name her son, interpreting for her the experience of being heard; she in turn named God, interpreting her experience of being seen.[31] Hagar—the exploited Egyptian slave girl, trafficked from her homeland, bedded by an octogenarian man (Gen. 16:16), and physically abused by his jealous wife—that invisible girl was seen by God. Out of a personal encounter between Abraham's God and an Egyptian trauma survivor, there arose personal theology.[32] And even though Hagar was never integrated into the lineage of the Israelites (in contrast with other non-Israelite women like Ruth or Tamar), her theologizing—affirming that the LORD is a God who sees the invisible and exploited—is canonized in Jewish Scripture.

Heavenly Figures: Daniel 7

Genesis 16 introduced the angel of the LORD as a mediating figure between God and humanity. In addition to the angel of the LORD, who represents

God in interactions with humans, the Old Testament speaks of the spirit of God not as a distinct divine person so much as an expression of the presence, wisdom, and power of the Lord (see, for example, Isa. 11:2; 63:10; Ps. 51:11; Gen. 1:2).[33] On the other end of the celestial spectrum, further away from the divine spirit and the divine-ish angel of the Lord, there exist the ordinary angels. Angels are nondivine supernatural beings in intertestamental Judaism and the New Testament, but at various points in the Hebrew Bible we perceive hints of their relationship to the old pagan idea of a divine counsel, the lesser deities of which have been downgraded in Israelite thought so they are no longer gods but mostly anonymous members of the heavenly host (see, for example, Gen. 11:6–7; Job 1:6; Ps. 82:1; 1 Kings 22:19–23). Israelite religion responded to polytheism by ascribing to YHWH some congenial names and attributes of pagan deities, while denying the reality of other gods and reconstruing the heavenly council in terms of a host of angels surrounding the Lord.

The complexity of the ways in which the Old Testament describes the heavenly host and the mediators of the Lord would create space for Christians to negotiate their unfolding development of the doctrines of the deity of Christ and the Trinity. But no text so lent itself to subsequent Christian hermeneutical innovation as did Daniel 7. In a nocturnal vision, Daniel witnesses the establishment of multiple thrones in heaven (Dan. 7:9). On one of them sits a white-haired and fiery God, surrounded by legions of celestial beings (7:10). God is called the "Ancient of Days," in keeping with descriptions of the Canaanite God 'El, who was called the "Ancient One" or "Father of Years."[34] This description also aligns thematically with the description of God as 'El 'Olam, the eternal God.[35]

Then, in verse 13, Daniel sees another figure with a human form, "one like a son of man" (*cəbar 'enosh, huios anthrōpou*) approaching the Ancient of Days while being borne along by clouds. In Canaanite religion, it was the god Ba'al, son of 'El, who rode on the clouds, so the Psalms sometimes attribute that mode of transport to YHWH (Ps. 68:4; 104:3), claiming for the Lord the majesty the pagans ascribed to Ba'al.[36] But in Daniel's vision the cloud rider like a son of man is distinct from and enthroned *alongside* the Ancient of Days, (much like Ba'al would have been seated alongside 'El). Moreover, to the figure like a son of man there is presented universal and eternal dominion. All of this was problematic for the sort of Jewish monotheism celebrated in the Shema (Deut. 6:4). But a few centuries later this crowded heavenly scene would serve as fodder for the theological speculations of a Jewish sect that came to think that their crucified Messiah might be divine.

Naming God in the New Testament

In the Greek New Testament we encounter a collection of writings, mostly authored by Jews, that grapple with unexpected experiences of divinity. Much like Hagar, who named God out of her experience of the Lord as the God who saw her, the earliest Christians felt that they had encountered God in Jesus and sought to name God in ways that interpreted their experiences as truly as they could without overtly violating their Jewish faith. While it would take centuries to systematize language to account for their high Christology and Trinitarian theology, the New Testament texts bear witness to the beginning of that process and provided the linguistic data that would shape patristic doctrinal formulations.

The Gospel of Mark provides insight into the ways that early Christians described the deity they perceived in Jesus, using three titles—Son of God, Son of Man, and Lord—all of which were extremely semantically elastic. The expression "Son of God" (Mark 1:1), for example, could be used to describe a normal human (Ps. 8:4; Ezek. 37:3), a divinely favored leader, like King David (Ps. 2:6–8), or a celestial being (Gen. 6:2, 4).[37] Similarly, the phrase "Son of Man" could refer simply to a human being (under the influence of Aramaic idiomatic usage), or it could be used as a Messianic title (under the influence of Dan. 7:13).[38] Finally, the word *kurios*, "lord," could just mean "boss" but was also the preferred Greek term for translating YHWH in the LXX.[39] The ambiguity of these terms afforded Christians some lexical leeway in communicating the divinity they perceived in Jesus.

Son of Man: Mark 2 and 14

This ambiguity is on full display in Mark 2, where the Pharisees criticize Jesus's disciples for gleaning on the Sabbath (an action that they understood as a violation of the commandment not to work on that day). Jesus responds by defending the disciples' participation in such life-sustaining activity, contending, "The sabbath was made for man, and not man for the sabbath" and then buttoning his argument with the daring statement, "so the Son of Man is *kurios* [L/lord] even of the sabbath" (v. 28).

Here polysemy is key to interpretation. Since the phrase "Son of Man" could be used as a synonym for "a human," and since *kurios* could just be understood as "boss," Jesus could just be interpreted as saying that the Sabbath should be a blessing for people, not a burden. But the reader of Mark knows (a) that Jesus uses "Son of Man" self-referentially;[40] (b) that *kurios* was the standard Greek translation of YHWH; and (c) that the Old Testament defines the Sabbath as God's.[41] All of this indicates that Jesus "shares with

God the identity as κύριος [*kurios*] of the sabbath."[42] Mark never affirms the Lordship of Christ to the exclusion of the Lordship of the heavenly God of whom Jesus speaks and to whom he relates. Rather, "There is one κύριος [*kurios*], and yet two figures, God and Jesus, share this name. . . . This, in Mark's view, does not compromise monotheism, but certainly reinterprets monotheism."[43]

At the end of his life, Jesus becomes rather less coy about his identity. Mark 14 narrates Jesus's interrogation by the Jewish high priest, who was hoping to get Jesus to admit to being a Messianic claimant—that is, an aspirant to the throne of Israel—so he could bring Jesus up on charges of political sedition before Pontius Pilate, his Roman overlord.[44] He asks, "Are you the Messiah, the son of the Blessed One?"[45]—revealing thereby the way in which the Messiah was often referred to with the title "Son of God," by analogy to David (Ps. 2:6–8).

Jesus's response, however, gives the high priest everything he wanted and a great deal more. He admits to being the Messiah by saying "I am," and then doubles down on that admission by interpreting his Messianic identity with an allusion to Daniel 7: "you will see the Son of Man seated at the right hand of the Power and coming with the clouds of heaven."[46] We have already discussed how Daniel 7 was a theological minefield since it implies divinity for a human-like figure. Jesus, however, barrels across that minefield, identifying himself with that godlike Messianic entity using the words *I am*, "I am," a phrase that evokes the name of God in Exodus 3:14 (*Egō eimi ho ōn*) and texts like Deuteronomy 32:39 (or Isa. 43:10; 46:4), in which God affirms "I am (*Egō eimi*) and there is no God except me."[47] In other words, when asked if he is the Davidic Messiah, Jesus responds, "If by 'Messiah' you mean a divine figure who will not only save Israel but be enthroned in heaven, then yes, I am that kind of God." The high priest picks up exactly what Jesus was putting down and condemns it as "Blasphemy!" (Mark 14:63–64).

Divine? Since When? Luke 1 and John 1

Later New Testament texts use names of God to affirm that Jesus's divinity extended back to the beginning of his human existence. For example, in Luke 1 the angel Gabriel announces that Mary will conceive the Messiah, despite her virginity, and that his kingdom would be unending, much like Daniel 7:14 indicated. The angel explains that her conception will be the result of an "overshadowing" by "the power of the Most High" (a.k.a. 'Elyon, a.k.a. the Holy Spirit). As such, her child would be called "Son of God" (Luke 1:35) and equivalently, *huios hupsistou*, "the Son of the Most High" (1:32). Even though the appellative "Son of God" could be used in a purely political Messianic sense, the angel indicates that Mary's child would in fact be Son of God in (for lack of a better term) "genetic" fashion.

Luke makes the divine identity of the baby more explicit when Mary hurries off to see her cousin, Elizabeth, who herself had just miraculously conceived a son, the prophet John. Under the inspiration of the Holy Spirit (v. 41), she recognizes what has happened in Mary and asks delightedly how she could be so blessed "that the mother of my Lord (*tou kuriou mou*) comes to me?" It is clear from Luke 1:38 and 46 that *kurios* is being used in reference to God, such that Jesus, who is conceived by God's Spirit, is likewise identified as God. As in Mark's Gospel, Jesus and God are both identified as *kurios* from Jesus's very conception, without collapsing the distinction between the two.[48]

John's gospel clarifies that the deity who became Jesus existed even prior to his conception, saying, "In the beginning was the *logos*, and the *logos* was with God, and the *logos* was God" (John 1:1). While this opening evokes various strands of Jewish religious language (divine wisdom, the *memra*, personification of the Torah, etc.[49]), this verse draws especially on the Stoic and Middle-Platonic philosophical use of the word *logos* to denote the divine active rational principle, which the Stoics believed organized and pervaded all creation.[50] John uses this term, already evocative of divinity, to affirm that, prior to the incarnation (v. 14), the *logos* (a) existed, (b) was God, and yet (c) was "with God" and therefore was somehow distinguishable from God. Being God and being distinguishable from God: this is basically the same antinomy that Luke and Mark express in their use of *kurios* for both God and Jesus.

John goes on to clarify that, contrary to what a Stoic conception of the *logos* could countenance, the *logos* became flesh in such a way that, in the *logos*, humans could witness the glory of God. John thus picks up the Old Testament belief that God's glory cannot be seen directly and contends that in Jesus all could see a semblance of God's glory. "No one" he says, "has ever seen God," at least not fully, and yet the *logos*, the "only begotten God (*monogenēs theos*) who is in the bosom of the Father, has made him known." John uses the language of Father and Son (1:14, 18) to characterize the relationship between *theos* and the *logos*.[51] The Old Testament only describes the Lord as Father on a few occasions, always indicating that the Father's children are humans, not deities.[52] But John reworks the terminology to communicate that God and the *logos* are conjointly divine, that, because of Jesus's filial relationship to the Father, the incarnate *logos* can authentically present God to and interpret God for (v. 18) humanity.

In brief, John 1 enhances the high Christology of the synoptic Gospels by adopting Old Testament (Father) and Stoic (*logos*) terms and reshaping their usage in innovative ways that articulate something of the mysterious relationship of *theos* with the person whom John knew as Jesus.

The Resurrected God: John 20 and Revelation 1

The baldest attribution of the title "God" to Jesus occurs in John 20, when the resurrected Christ appears to the disciples and Thomas cries out, "My Lord and my God."[53] Although the gospel opened with the assertion that the *logos* was with and was itself *theos*. Thomas explicitly ascribes to Jesus both the titles of *kurios* and *theos*. Nonetheless, this application of deity to Jesus does not collapse the Godhead into Jesus; for, when Jesus appeared to the women disciples a week earlier, Jesus had told them, "I am ascending to my Father and your Father, to my God and your God" (John 20:17), thus maintaining a clear distinction between himself and God the Father.

The interplay between divine names and attributes of the resurrected Christ becomes more elaborate in the book of Revelation, when the Seer has a vision of God in the heavenly throne room. In keeping with the Old Testament, the Seer refers to God as the Almighty, the Pantocrator (Rev. 1:8), a Septuagint term used to translate Shaddai in Job and Yahweh Tzebaoth in the Former and Latter Prophets. He also calls God the Alpha and Omega (Rev. 1:4), emphasizing the Lord's eternity in accordance with the Old Testament description of God as the Ancient of Days and 'El 'Olam.

Thereafter, the Seer claps eyes on Jesus, who appears with characteristics both of an angelic being (especially as per Dan. 10:5), and of God (especially as per Dan. 7).[54] The Seer describes him as "one like a Son of Man," which calls to mind Daniel 7's description of the celestial enthronement of such a figure. But whereas Daniel saw one like a son of man being presented *before* the Ancient of Days, here that figure is described *very much like* the Ancient of Days. Like the Ancient of Days, his hair is bright white (Rev. 1:14; Dan. 7:9); his eyes are like a flame of fire, just as fire flowed from the presence of the Ancient of Days (Rev. 1:14; Dan. 7:10). Further, when the Son of Man introduces himself, he uses the formula *egō eimi*, "I am," calling to mind the name of the Lord from Exodus 3:14 and Isaiah 43:10, 46:4.[55] And if one were initially uncertain whether such an allusion was intended through the *egō eimi* phrase, the Son of Man then predicates of himself the very attributes of eternity the Lord had just claimed in 1:8. So although the divine names in this text (Almighty, Alpha and Omega, Lord) are applied primarily to the Father (a title used in 1:6), the resurrected Son of Man is attributed the characteristics corresponding to those names, reinforcing his incorporation in the Christian understanding of God.

The Name Above Every Name: Philippians 2

Revelation 1 is not the only text that underscores both the preexistence and future reign of the Son; Paul does the same in a way that is even more explicit about the application of the divine name to Jesus.

As part of an exhortation to the Philippian believers to prioritize the needs of others over their own (Phil. 2:1–5), Paul invokes how the preexistent Christ took on humanity and allowed himself to be crucified (2:6–8) such that God consequently exalted Jesus and "gave him the name that is above every name" (2:9). As every Jew knew, the name above every name is Yahweh, and that point is made utterly clear in verse 10, when Paul cites something that the prophet Isaiah said about Yahweh.[56]

In the book of Isaiah, the uniqueness of the name of the Lord is repeatedly celebrated (41:13; 42:8; 43:11; 44:5; 45:18).[57] God declares, "I am the Lord, that is my name; my glory I give to no other" (Isa. 42:8).[58] God swears that eventually "all the ends of the earth" (45:22) will recognize the Lord as the only true God. "To me," he says in Isaiah 45:3, "every knee will bow, every tongue shall swear." It is this text that Paul applies to Jesus (Phil. 2:10–11), declaring that the fulfillment of the expectation (in Isaiah 45) of YHWH's universal dominion comes precisely in universal submission to Jesus Christ as Lord (*kurios Iēsous Christos*; Phil 2:11). As in the Gospels, YHWH does not cease to be *kurios* by naming Jesus as *kurios*; both share the title of being the one *kurios* (again, bear in mind Isa. 42:8), and for that reason the exaltation of Jesus is precisely for the glory of God the Father (Phil. 2:11).[59]

The Son with the Father and the Spirit: Matthew 28 and John 14

We are finally in a position to examine how "Spirit" emerges as a name for God, which transpires in conjunction with the attribution of divine names to Jesus, as Christians discerned that Jesus related to God not only as the Father but also and distinctly as the Spirit.

To be clear: attributing deity to the Spirit of the Lord was not a Christian innovation; the Old Testament speaks often of God's Spirit. Early Christianity, however, differentiates the Spirit from the Father. So at the end of Matthew's gospel, the risen Christ declares to his followers, "All authority in heaven and on earth has been given to me" (Matt. 28:18[60]), thus alluding to Daniel 7:14, in which the Son of Man received dominion over all the nations of the world. He then tells the disciples to teach others to obey him, baptizing them "in the name of the Father and of the Son and of the Holy Spirit."[61] This bespeaks a distinction between the Spirit and the Father, just as the Son was distinct from the Father and Spirit.

Since the Father and Spirit were always considered divine, baptizing in Jesus's name as well as theirs implies that Jesus is also divine. What is odd in this instruction, however, is the singular "name," *onoma*, in the phrase "in the name of the Father and of the Son and of the Holy Spirit." One would expect the plural *onomata*, "names," if the baptism were to be performed in the three discrete names of Father, Son, and Spirit. The singular "name" suggests the shared identity of Father, Son, and Spirit, and perhaps even implies baptism into the one name the Father gave to Jesus (Phil. 2:9; John 17:11): the name of the Lord, YHWH.[62]

The commissioning of the disciples concludes with the promise "I am with you always, to the end of the age" (Matt. 28:20), alluding to one other name for Jesus: Emmanuel, a Hebrew name from Isaiah 7:14, meaning "God (is/be) with us." Prior to Jesus's birth, the angel of the Lord declared that Jesus's conception was "from the Holy Spirit" (Matt. 1:20) such that Jesus should be called "God is with us" (Matt. 1:23) because in the incarnation God came to dwell bodily with Israel. Matthew's gospel therefore concludes with the promise that, even after Jesus's resurrection, he did not desert his followers.

The (logical) worry that Jesus might have abandoned the disciples after his death also pops up in John 14 (vv. 2–3, 13). There Jesus reveals that in his impending death (John 13:31–38) he would proceed to the Father, which emboldens Philip to request, "Lord, show us the Father." To this Jesus replies (in accordance with John 1:18; 14:6–7), "Whoever has seen me has seen the Father," thus confirming the unity of Jesus and the Father.[63] This unity is so robust that Jesus affirms that when the disciples would later invoke Jesus's name and Jesus would act on their behalf, the Father would thereby be glorified in the Son (John 14:13–14; the logic is similar to that behind Phil. 2:11), for Jesus had come in the name of the Father (John 5:43; 10:25).[64]

John then adds an additional dimension to this intradivine relationality. Jesus clarifies that after his death the Father would send the Advocate (*paraklētos*, cf. 16:7), the Holy Spirit, to accompany the disciples (14:26).[65] That Spirit would be sent, however, not in the name of the Father (as Jesus was), but in the name of Jesus himself in a way that both reinforces John's representation of the Son as part of God and uses "Holy Spirit" as a name for an entity of the one God distinguishable from the Father and the Son.[66] As Gary Burge says, "The rudimentary Trinitarian implications of 14:25–26 are inescapable."[67] It would of course take centuries for terms like "hypostasis," "person," "substance," and "essence" to coalesce and then to be used in coherent and agreed-upon fashions. But before Christians had technical dogmatic theological terminology for God as Trinity, they had names for

God as Father, Son, Holy Spirit, and Lord. Naming God is theologizing. And theologizing, as I have said, is dangerous business.

Continuing to Name God?

This chapter has examined how the Jewish Scriptures unfold their understanding of the Lord and ascribe to God certain names of Canaanite deities. Although the Lord was Israel's covenant God, they accepted that non-Israelites like Melchizedek and Balaam could also speak truly about YHWH. This study has also examined how Christians named God. They were deeply rooted in the Jewish Scriptures and yet they were shaped by their personal experiences of Jesus and the Holy Spirit and drew on their knowledge of pagan ideas such as the Stoic *logos*. The names they ascribed to God were the raw material of what became Trinitarian orthodoxy. If the early Christians were right about Jesus, they had glimpsed more than Rabbi Akiba had done in his celestial vision. Akiba, however, would have lumped them in with "The Other Guy."

But what does this mean for those of us who are Christians, knowing that Muslim friends name God differently than we do? The passage that I keep coming back to is the story of Hagar, the mother of Ishmael, the ancestor of Muhammad. Like Moses, like Isaiah, like John the Seer, she claps eyes on the Lord. But unlike them, she creates a name for God out of her own experience. And even though Hagar and her descendants are not made part of Israel, Israel canonizes her naming of God, her theology. The key question for us today is whether those of us who understand ourselves as, ethnically or spiritually, children of Sarah ought to listen to how God has been named by the children of Hagar and agree that they too have seen God.[68]

Notes

1. The "–im" ending is typically a plural suffix in Hebrew, but it is widely agreed that in the Hebrew Bible, when Elohim refers to the God of Israel, the plural ending does not indicate plurality in God, even if it may reflect polytheistic antecedents and was subsequently exploited by Christian interpreters for Trinitarian ends.

2. See William VanGemeren, ed., *New International Dictionary of Old Testament Theology & Exegesis*, 5 vols. (hereafter, *NIDOTTE*) (Grand Rapids, MI: Zondervan Academic, 1997), 1:257–58, 275. Adonai is sometimes used in construct forms such as "Lord of all the earth" (Josh. 3:13; Ps. 97:5; Mic. 4:13) or "Lord of lords" (Deut. 10:17; Ps. 136:3).

3. *NIDOTTE* 4:1295–1300. YHWH, in some places, is more briefly Yah. Clifford Hubert Durousseau, "Yah: A Name of God," *Jewish Bible Quarterly* 42, no. 1 (2014): 21–26.

4. Koog-Pyoung Hong, "The Euphemism for the Ineffable Name of God and its Early Evidence in Chronicles," *Journal for the Study of the Old Testament* 37, no. 4 (2013): 473–84.

5. Sometimes the Tetragrammaton was vocalized as Elohim or even Hashem (literally, "The Name").

6. See R. Laird Harris, "The Pronunciation of the Tetragram," *Presbyterion* 7, no. 1–2 (1981): 173–75; and George Howard, "The Tetragram and the New Testament," *Journal of Biblical Literature* 96, no. 1 (1977): 63–76.

7. It is unwise to press the philological details of the correspondence between the name YHWH and the phrase *'ehyeh 'asher 'ehyeh*. Harris, "The Pronunciation of the Tetragram," 178–79. For an overview of interpretations of the phrase's meaning, see, e.g., Charles R. Gianotti, "The Meaning of the Divine Name YHWH," *Bibliotheca Sacra* 142, no. 565 (1985): 41–46; and Victor P. Hamilton, *Exodus: An Exegetical Commentary* (Grand Rapids, MI: Baker Academic, 2011), 64.

8. Hebrew imperfect verbs can be translated in the present tense but are more frequently rendered in the future.

9. Amitai Adler, "What's in a Name? Reflections upon Divine Names and the Attraction of God to Israel," *Jewish Bible Quarterly* 37, no. 4 (2009): 265–68.

10. On being the covenant God of Israel: "This name. . . identifies God as that ultimate mystery who is free to be whoever and whatever God chooses to be. . . . Even deeper than the mystery of absolute freedom is the mystery in which such freedom binds itself . . . in faithfulness to a particular community to which it has made promises that it now undertakes to fulfill." J. Gerald Janzen, *Exodus*, Westminster Bible Companion (Louiville, KY: Westminster John Knox, 1997), 34. On fulfilling the vows made to Israel's ancestors, see Gianotti, "The Meaning of the Divine Name YHWH," 44–48; and J. Gerald Janzen, "What's in a Name? Yahweh in Exodus 3 and the Wider Biblical Context," *Interpretation* 33, no. 3 (1979): 233–34.

11. For example, in Exodus 6:6–8, God declares Godself to be Yahweh and then promises to free Israel from Egypt, to take them as God's covenant people, and to give them the promised land, three times in those verses repeating "I am YHWH." Gianotti, "The Meaning of the Divine Name YHWH," 46; Janzen, *Exodus*, 53; Brevard Childs, *The Book of Exodus: A Critical, Theological Commentary*, Old Testament Library (Philadelphia: Westminster John Knox, 1974), 115; and Hamilton, *Exodus*, 101.

12. This idea is expressed elsewhere in the Old Testament as well: Genesis 16:13; Deuteronomy 4:12; Psalms 97:2.

13. See also Numbers 12:8; Deuteronomy 34:10; cf. Genesis 32:30 (Jacob); Exodus 24:9–11 (Aaron and the seventy-two elders); Isaiah 6:1–5 (Isaiah). Hamilton, *Exodus*, 569.

14. While the punctuation of the NRSV implies that 33:19 and 34:6–7 are simply statements subsequent to the divine name, it is more satisfactory to see them as expositions of what it means for God to be YHWH, especially given the repetition of the verb *vayiqra*, "to call" or "to call out," both before the bare statement of the name of the Lord in 34:5 and before the more expansive repetition of the name of the Lord in combination with the description a "God merciful and gracious" in 34:6.

15. See Childs, *Exodus*, 596.

16. The joint affirmation that God will forgive iniquity and yet punish the guilty appears across the Old Testament (Num. 14:18; Neh. 9:17; Ps. 86:15). Childs, *Exodus*, 612.

17. Numbers 24:15–16; Deuteronomy 32:8; Psalms 7:19, 47:2, 92:2; Genesis 14:19–20.

18. Walter R. Wifall, "El Shaddai or El of the Fields," *Zeitschrift für die alttestamentliche Wissenschaft* 92, no. 1 (1980): 24; *NIDOTTE* 1:400–401; W. Sibley Towner, *Genesis*, Westminster Bible Companion (Louisville, KY: Westminster John Knox, 2001), 147; and R. N. Whybray, "Genesis," in *The Oxford Bible Commentary*, eds. John Barton and John Muddiman (Oxford: Oxford University Press, 2001), 50. *'Elyon* was perhaps also epithet for *'El*; Robert Alter, *The Five Books of Moses: A Translation with Commentary* (New York: Norton, 2004), 72; and Gordon Wenham, *Genesis 1–15*, Word Biblical Commentary (Dallas: Word, 1998), 317.

19. Whybray, "Genesis," 50; and Wenham, *Genesis 1–15*, 317.

20. Childs, *Exodus*, 110; and Hamilton, *Exodus*, 99. Many argue that the term means "mountain," while others associate it with *saddai*, "open field." Wifall, "El Shaddai," 24–32.

21. 1 Samuel 15:2; 17:45; 2 Samuel 6:2; 1 Kings 19:14; 2 Kings 19:31; Psalms 46:7, 11; Isaiah 6:3, 5; and James 5:4. *Yahweh Tzebaoth* is translated *kurios sabaōth* or *kurios tōn dynameōn* in the LXX; see *NIDOTTE* 4:1297–1298.

22. Harriet Lutzky, "Shadday as a Goddess Epithet," *Vetus Testamentum* 48, no. 1 (1998): 15–36; and Christopher B. Hays, "'Can a Woman Forget Her Nursing Child?' Divine Breastfeeding and the God of Israel," in *Divine Doppelgängers: YHWH's Ancient Look-Alikes*, ed. Collin Cornell (University Park: Pennsylvania State University Press, 2020), 202–14.

23. See, for example, Isaiah 42:14, 49:14–15, and 66:12–13; see also, in the New Testament, Matthew 23:37; Luke 13:34, although drawing on language about God in Psalms 36:7, 57:1, 63:7, 91:4.

24. Jared C. Hood, "I Appeared as El Shaddai: Intertextual Interplay in Exodus 6:3," *Westminster Theological Journal* 76, no. 1 (2014): 176–79.

25. In spite of Old Testament orthodoxy, archaeology indicates that popular Israelite practice may have represented Asherah at times as a consort of YHWH. William G. Dever, "Asherah, Consort of Yahweh? New Evidence from Kuntillet 'Arjûd," *Bulletin of the American Schools of Oriental Research* 255 (1984): 21–37.

26. Interestingly, v. 14 refers to the place as a well, *bəʿer*, not a spring. The distinction here is not incidental. Rather, the text engages in a telling wordplay, for the word for *spring*, *ʿayin*, also means *eye*; likewise, the place name, Shur, is a homophone for the verb *shur*, which means "to see, gaze on." Towner, *Genesis*, 161.

27. Gerhard von Rad, *Genesis: A Commentary*, trans. John H. Marks, Old Testament Library (Philadelphia: Westminster John Knox, 1972), 193–94; cf. Hermann Gunkel, *Genesis*, trans. Mark E. Biddle, Mercer Library of Biblical Studies (Macon, GA: Mercer University Press, 1997), 186–87.

28. For example, in Exodus 4:24, the Masoretic Text (the traditional Hebrew text) says that YHWH appeared in front of Moses and tried to kill him, but the LXX changes it to the *aggelos kuriou* (Gunkel, *Genesis*, 186), probably to avoid the idea that Moses and Zipporah saw God directly.

29. Rad, *Genesis*, 193.

30. *Rō'iy* is an odd phrase, but seems to be composed of the divine epithet El in combination with something like the participle of *ra'ah* (to see) and a first-person singular suffix, hence: "The God Seeing Me." It is easier to see the grammar underlying the related etymology of "Beer–lahai–roi" (Gen. 16:14), "The Well of the Living One Who Sees Me."

31. James Chukwuma Okoye, "Sarah and Hagar: Genesis 16 and 21," *Journal for the Study of the Old Testament* 32, no. 2 (2007): 168–69.

32. I am grateful to Dr. Carly Crouch for this insight.

33. For an overview of the way the Spirit of God is construed in the Old Testament and intertestamental Judaism, see Gordon D. Fee, *God's Empowering Presence: The Holy Spirit in the Letters of Paul* (Peabody, MA: Hendrickson, 1994), 905–15.

34. P. R. Davies, "Daniel," in *The Oxford Bible Commentary*, eds. John Barton and John Muddiman (Oxford: Oxford University Press, 2001), 567; John H. Walton, Victor H. Matthews, and Mark W. Chavalas, *The IVP Bible Background Commentary: Old Testament* (Downers Grove: InterVarsity, 2000), 741; and *NIDOTTE* 3:346.

35. Genesis 21:33. Compare Jeremiah 10:10; Isaiah 26:4. See *NIDOTTE* 3:346.

36. Walton, Matthews, and Chavalas, *Bible Background Commentary*, 741.

37. The term is clearly Messianic in, for example, Luke 4:41; John 1:49.

38. See discussion in Darrell L. Bock, "Son of Man," in *Dictionary of Jesus and the Gospels*, eds. Joel B. Green, Jeannine K. Brown, and Nicholas Perrin (Downer's Grove, IL: InterVarsity Academic, 2013), 894–900.

39. Ceslas Spicq, *Theological Lexicon of the New Testament*, 3 vols. (Peabody, MA: Hendrickson, 1994), 2:347, 3:1058–81. It was also an appellative for pagan deities; see, for example, Exodus 14:4, 15:26; Leviticus 11:44, 19:3–4; Deuteronomy 5:6–9; Hosea 13:4; Isaiah 43:3, 51:15; Psalms 81[80]:10. Note that the Hebrew Masoretic text and the Septuagint differ in their approaches to numbering the Psalms. Both systems are in use today. Hence, the text mentioned here is cited according to both systems.

40. 2:10, 8:31, 8:38, 9:9, 9:12, 9:31, and so on.

41. Exodus 16:25, 20:10, 31:13; Leviticus 19:3, 19:30; Deuteronomy 5:14; Ezekiel 20:12–13. R. T. France, *The Gospel of Mark*, New International Greek Testament Commentary (Grand Rapids, MI: Eerdmans, 2002), 148.

42. Daniel Johansson, "*Kyrios* in the Gospel of Mark," *Journal for the Study of the New Testament* 33:1 (2010): 112. For other places where Jesus is called Lord in ways that identify him with YHWH, see Acts 8:16; 1 Corinthians 12:3; Romans 1:3–4, 10:9–13.

43. Johansson, "*Kyrios*," 119.

44. The Jewish temple leadership knew that Pilate would not be bothered by any of Jesus's alleged theological heterodoxy, but if Pilate were to believe Jesus to be a claimant to the throne of David, then Caesar's governor in Judea would be forced to take swift action.

45. The phrase "The Blessed One" is a circumlocution for the name of God, reflecting the first century practice of not naming God directly. Harris, "The Pronunciation of the Tetragram," 174; and R. Kendall Soulen, "Jesus and the Divine Name," *Union Seminary Quarterly Review* 65, no. 1–2 (2015): 50–53.

46. The term *Power* serves as a circumlocution for the divine name. France, *The Gospel of Mark*, 610, 13.

47. On the background of the "I am" sayings, see Grant Macaskill, "Name Christology, Divine Aseity, and the I Am Sayings in the Fourth Gospel," *Journal of Theological Interpretation* 12, no. 2 (2018): 223–30. Ironically, this phrase is slightly circumlocutious; Jesus engages in a bit of the reverential name avoidance appropriate to the divine name even as he applies it to himself. Soulen, "Jesus and the Divine Name," 55–56. The Gospel of John uses the phrase "I am" in similar ways: John 4:25–26, 6:20, 8:24, 6:28, 6:58, 13:19, 18:14; see further Soulen, "Jesus and the Divine Name," 53–55.

48. Argued in detail in C. Kavin Rowe, *Early Narrative Christology: The Lord in the Gospel of Luke* (Grand Rapids, MI: Baker Academic, 2009), 31–49.

49. Macaskill, "Name Christology," 231.

50. See, for example, Diogenes Laertius, *Vit.* 7.134–38; and C. H. Dodd, *The Interpretation of the Fourth Gospel* (London: SPCK, 1968), 280.

51. Although these terms are used in various parts of the New Testament (see, for example, Mark 14:36; Romans 8:15; Galatians 4:6), they are especially pervasive in Matthew and Luke, most poignantly in the Lord's Prayer (Matt. 6:9; Luke 11:2).

52. Fifteen times; see, for example, Jeremiah 3:4, 19; Isaiah 63:16, 64:8; see *NIDOTTE* 4:1299.

53. In the Old Testament, Lord and God are often used as synonyms and even in pairs, as in, for example, the construction *'elohi YHWH* ("the Lord my God"), as in Psalms 7:2, 7:4 in the Masoretic Text, 30:3; René Kieffer, "John," in *The Oxford Bible Commentary*, eds. John Barton and John Muddiman (Oxford: Oxford University Press, 2001), 998.

54. For details, see Brandon D. Smith, "The Identification of Jesus with YHWH in the Book of Revelation: A Brief Sketch," *Criswell Theological Review* 14, no. 1 (2016): 75–78; David E. Aune, *Revelation 1–5*, Word Biblical Commentary (Dallas: Word, 1997), 94–97; and G. K. Beale, *The Book of Revelation: A Commentary on the Greek Text*, New International Greek Testament Commentary (Grand Rapids, MI: Eerdmans, 1999), 209–15.

55. "I am" language occurs in Revelations 1:8, 1:17, 2:23, 21:6, 22:16, where it "is used to make divine predications of the speaker." Aune, *Revelation 1–5*, 100–101. See also Macaskill, "Name Christology," 226–28.

56. For an overview of key issues, see Peter T. O'Brien, *The Epistle to the Philippians: A Commentary on the Greek Text*, New International Greek Testament Commentary (Grand Rapids, MI: Eerdmans, 1991), 238.

57. G. Walter Hansen, *The Letter to the Philippians*, Pillar New Testament Commentary (Grand Rapids, MI: Eerdmans, 2009), 163.

58. This causes one to think of another name for God, 'El Qannah, the Jealous God; Exodus 34:14; cf. Exodus 20:5; Deuteronomy 4:24, 5:9, 6:15.

59. Cf. Gerald F. Hawthorne, *Philippians*, Word Biblical Commentary (Dallas: Word, 1983), 94; and O'Brien, *Philippians*, 251.

60. As also affirmed in Philemon 2:10–11.

61. The triadic combination of Father, Son, and Spirit is found in 1 Corinthians 6:11, 12:4–6; 2 Corinthians 12:13; Galatians 4:6; 1 Peter 1:2. Ulrich Luz, *Matthew 21–28: A Commentary*, Hermeneia (Minneapolis: Augsburg Fortress, 2005), 632.

62. W. D. Davies and Dale C. Allison, *A Critical and Exegetical Commentary on the*

Gospel According to Saint Matthew, 3 vols., International Critical Commentary (Edinburgh: T&T Clark, 1997), 3:685–86.

63. In John 10:30, 37–38, Jesus had said "I and the Father are one."

64. John goes on to claim that the Father had given Jesus his name (John 17:11–12, 26). Soulen, "Jesus and the Divine Name," 53–54.

65. Probably the most adequate translation of *paraklētos* is "advocate," with a legal nuance, insofar as John 15:26 and 16:7–11 use the term, in relationship to testimony and judgment (cf. Mark 13:11; Luke 12:11–12). Gerhard Friedrich, ed., *Theological Dictionary of the New Testament*, vol. 5, trans. Geoffrey W. Bromiley (Grand Rapids, MI: Eerdmans, 1967), 813–14; D. A. Carson, *The Gospel According to John*, The Pillar New Testament Commentary (Leicester: Intervarsity, 1991), 499; and Gary M. Burge, *John*, NIV Application Commentary (Grand Rapids, MI: Zondervan, 2000), 395–96. John 16:7, in complementary fashion, says that Jesus will send the Spirit (16:7). First Peter 1:11 accordingly calls the Holy Spirit, "The Spirit of Christ."

66. George R. Beasley-Murray, *John*, 2nd ed., Word Biblical Commentary (Nashville: Thomas Nelson, 1999), 261; and Carson, *The Gospel According to John*, 505.

67. Burge, *John*, 398–99.

68. During the closing plenary of 2021 Building Bridges Seminar, a participant asked whether I would genuinely maintain that Hagar is the only person in the Bible to have named God—pointing out that the Psalmists give names to God. I replied that, of course, the Scripture is constantly predicating names for God—making up names for God. Enscripturation almost by its nature entails applying names to God. However, in the *narration* of Scriptural events, Hagar is unique as a person insofar as she is described as creating a name for God. Hagar does something that Moses does not do, that Isaiah does not do, that John the Seer does not do. So within the narrative world represented by the Bible, she is unique.

2

Bible Passages on Naming God

Selections for Dialogue

The passages collected here are according to the New Revised Standard Version.[1] *The bracketed words are provided to clarify the names of God in use in these verses.*

Genesis 14:18–19

[18]And King Melchizedek of Salem . . . was priest of God Most High ['El 'Elyon]. [19]He blessed him and said, "Blessed be Abram by God Most High ['El 'Elyon], maker of heaven and earth!"

Genesis 16:7, 9–11, 13–14

[7]The angel of the Lord found [Hagar] by a spring of water in the wilderness, the spring on the way to Shur. . . . [9]The angel of the Lord said to
her, "Return to your mistress, and submit to her." [10]The angel of the Lord
also said to her. . . . "I will so greatly multiply your offspring that they
cannot be counted for multitude." [11]And the angel of the Lord said to her,

"Now you have conceived and shall bear a son;
you shall call him Ishmael,
for the Lord has given heed to your affliction. . . ."

[13]So she named the Lord who spoke to her, "You are 'El-roi" [The God
Who Sees Me]; for she said, 'Have I really seen God and remained alive
after seeing him?' [14]Therefore the well was called Beer-lahai-roi [Well of
the Living One Who Sees Me].

Genesis 35:11

God said to [Jacob], "I am God Almighty ['El Shaddai]: be fruitful and multiply; a nation and a company of nations shall come from you, and kings shall spring from you."

Genesis 49:24–25

24[Joseph's] arms were made agile by the hands of the Mighty One of
Jacob, by the name of the Shepherd, the Rock of Israel, 25by the God of
your father, who will help you, by the Almighty [Shaddai] who will bless
you with blessings of heaven above, blessings of the deep that lies beneath,
blessings of the breasts and of the womb.

Exodus 3:13–15

13But Moses said to God [Elohim], "If I come to the Israelites and say to
them, 'The God of your ancestors has sent me to you,' and they ask me,
'What is his name?' what shall I say to them?" 14God said to Moses, "I
AM WHO I AM [*'ehyeh 'asher 'ehyeh*]." He said further, "Thus you shall say
to the Israelites, 'I AM [YHWH] has sent me to you.'" 15God also said to
Moses, "Thus you shall say to the Israelites, 'The LORD, the God [Elohim]
of your ancestors, the God of Abraham, the God of Isaac, and the God of
Jacob, has sent me to you':

This is my name for ever,
and this my title for all generations."

Exodus 33:18–20; 34:5–6

18Moses said, "Show me your glory, I pray." 19And he said, "I will make
all my goodness pass before you, and will proclaim before you the name,
'The LORD' [YHWH]; and I will be gracious to whom I will be gracious,
and will show mercy on whom I will show mercy. 20But," he said, "you
cannot see my face; for no one shall see me and live.". . .

5The LORD descended in the cloud and stood with him there, and proclaimed the name, "The LORD." 6The LORD passed before him, and proclaimed,

"The LORD, the LORD,
a God merciful and gracious,
slow to anger,
and abounding in steadfast love and faithfulness. . . ."

Numbers 24:15–16

[15]The oracle of Balaam son of Beor, the oracle of the man whose eye is
clear, [16]the oracle of one who hears the words of God [El], and knows the
knowledge of the Most High [Elyon], who sees the vision of the Almighty
[Shaddai].

Isaiah 6:1–3, 5

[1]I saw the Lord [*Adonai*] sitting on a throne, high and lofty. . . . [2]Seraphs
were in attendance above him. . . . [3]And one called to another and said:
"Holy, holy, holy is the LORD of hosts [YHWH Tzebaoth]; the whole
earth is full of his glory." . . . [5]And I said: "Woe is me! I am lost, for I am a
man of unclean lips, and I live among a people of unclean lips; yet my eyes
have seen the King, the LORD of hosts [YHWH Tzebaoth]!"

Daniel 7:9, 13–14

[9]As I watched, thrones were set in place, and an Ancient of Days took his
throne, his clothing was white as snow, and the hair of his head like pure
wool; his throne was fiery flames. . . . [13]I saw one like a son of man [*kibar
'anash; huios anthropou*] coming with the clouds of heaven. And he came
to the Ancient of Days and was presented before him. [14]To him was given
dominion and glory and kingship, that all peoples, nations, and languages
should serve him. His dominion is an everlasting dominion that shall not
pass away, and his kingship is one that shall never be destroyed.

Matthew 28:17–20

[17]When [the disciples] saw [Jesus], they worshiped him. . . . [18]And Jesus
came and said to them, "All authority in heaven and on earth has been
given to me. [19]Go therefore and make disciples of all nations, baptizing
them in the name of the Father and of the Son and of the Holy Spirit,
[20]and teaching them to obey everything that I have commanded you. And
remember, I am with you always, to the end of the age."

Mark 2:27–28

[27]Then he said to them, "The sabbath was made for man, and not man
for the sabbath; [28]so the Son of Man/son of man is Lord/lord even of the
sabbath."

Mark 14:61–64[2]

[61]The high priest asked him, "Are you the Messiah, the Son of the Blessed One?" [62]Jesus said, "I am; and

> 'you will see the Son of Man seated at the right hand of the Power,'
> and 'coming with the clouds of heaven.'"

[63]Then the high priest tore his clothes and said, "Why do we still need witnesses? [64]You have heard his blasphemy!"

Luke 1:30–35

[30]The angel said to her. . . , [31]"You will conceive in your womb and bear a son, and you will name him Jesus. [32]He will be great, and will be called the Son of the Most High, and the Lord God will give to him the throne of his ancestor David. [33]He will reign over the house of Jacob forever, and of his kingdom there will be no end." [34]Mary said to the angel, "How can this be, since I am a virgin?" [35]The angel said to her, "The Holy Spirit will come upon you, and the power of the Most High will overshadow you; therefore the child to be born will be holy; he will be called Son of God."

John 1:1, 14, 18

[1]In the beginning was the Word [Logos], and the Word was with God, and the Word was God. . . . [14]And the Word became flesh and lived among us, and we have seen his glory, the glory as the only begotten of the Father full of grace and truth. . . . [18]No one has ever seen God. The only begotten God, who is close to the Father's heart, has made him known.

John 14:8–10, 13, 25–26

[8]Philip said to him, "Lord, show us the Father, and we will be satisfied." [9]Jesus said to him, "Have I been with you all this time, Philip, and you still do not know me? Whoever has seen me has seen the Father. . . . [10]Do you not believe that I am in the Father and the Father is in me? . . . [13]I will do whatever you ask in my name, so that the Father may be glorified in the Son. . . . [25]I have said these things to you while I am still with you. [26]But the Advocate [Parakletos], the Holy Spirit, whom the Father will send in my name, will teach you everything."

John 20:27–28

27[Jesus] said to Thomas, "Put your finger here and see my hands. Reach out your hand and put it in my side. Do not doubt but believe." 28Thomas answered him, "My Lord and my God!"

Philippians 2:5–11

5Let the same mind be in you that was in Christ Jesus, 6who, though he
was in the form of God, did not regard equality with God as something
to be exploited, 7but emptied himself, taking the form of a slave, being
born in human likeness. And being found in human form, 8he humbled
himself and became obedient to the point of death—even death on a
cross. 9Therefore God also highly exalted him and gave him the name that
is above every name, 10so that at the name of Jesus every knee should bend,
in heaven and on earth and under the earth, 11and every tongue should
confess that Jesus Christ is Lord, to the glory of God the Father.

Revelation 1:8, 13–15, 17–18

8"I am the Alpha and the Omega," says the Lord God, who is and who was
and who is to come, the Almighty [Pantokrator]. . . . 13I saw one like the
Son of Man. . . . 14His head and his hair were white as white wool, white
as snow; his eyes were like a flame of fire, 15his feet were like burnished
bronze, refined as in a furnace, and his voice was like the sound of many
waters. . . . 17When I saw him, I fell at his feet as though dead. But he
placed his right hand on me, saying, "Do not be afraid; I am the first and
the last, 18and the living one. I was dead, and see, I am alive forever and
ever; and I have the keys of Death and of Hades."

Note

1. The New Revised Standard Version of the Bible, copyright 1989 by the Division of Christian Education of the National Council of the Churches of Christ in the USA (used by permission; all rights reserved).

2. See also Luke 22:67–71 and Matt. 26:63–66.

3

Calling God by His Names

The Subject and Object of "Naming God" in the Qur'an

Maria Massi Dakake

To God belong the most beautiful names, so call Him by them. Q. 7:180
Call upon God, or call upon the Compassionate. Whichever you call upon, to Him belong the most beautiful Names. Q. 17:110

God possesses the "most beautiful names" (*al-asmā' al-ḥusnā*), the Qur'an tells us more than once. All of these beautiful names, for Muslims, come from the Qur'an—that is, from God's own speech. They are the names He has given Himself. By revealing them in the Qur'an (and in other revelations), He has "spoken" His own names to human beings that they might speak those names back to Him. He not only allows and encourages human beings to call Him by His name, but in the Qur'an He offers multiple names by which human beings might "name" God and supplicate Him. The theme of the 2021 Building Bridges Seminar was "Naming God." God is the object in this phrase, but from a Qur'anic perspective, He is also the subject. God is both the named and the one who names. In the biblical book of Genesis, God allows Adam to give names to God's various other creations (Gen. 2:19, 3:20). In the Qur'an, Adam is given no such power of naming at all; rather, it is God who teaches Adam all of "the names."[1] From the Qur'anic perspective, since God reserves the power of naming exclusively for Himself in the Qur'an, and He alone authorizes the names that His creatures may use to call upon Him, there could hardly be a vainer act on the part of human beings than to either assign God's Name to other things (essentially the sin of "associationism" or *shirk*) or to seek to call upon God by names of one's own devising. We might even ask to what extent there is a difference between these two.

In the Qur'an, such false naming is implicitly compared to idolatry—that is, worshipping objects of one's own manufacture. Like idolatry, calling God by names of one's own devising is not discussed primarily as an act of heresy on the part of human beings but as an act of futility. The emphasis is not so much on such acts as an affront to God—who, the Qur'an assures us, suffers no harm as a result of human actions—but as acts without even any fleeting efficacy for human beings that might slightly offset the eternal harm it will cause them. When the Qur'an condemns false worship, it frequently derides it as the worship of "mere names that you have named," and "[names] for which God has sent down no authority."[2] Since God both *names* and *teaches* the names of all things He has brought into being, to worship "names that you have named," is to worship nothing at all. This may not be "idol worship" in the crassest sense—that is, it may not involve material idols—but it is, at the very least, "idle worship"—useless, vain, and empty.

God is one, the Qur'an affirms without reservation, but His names are multiple—and to deepen the apparent paradox, among the many names for God in the Qur'an is the name "the One" (al-Wāḥid/al-Aḥad). The Qur'an refers both to God's Name (singular) and to God's Name*s* (plural). For example, all Qur'anic verses (but one) begin "in the Name of God, the Compassionate, the Merciful" (with "name" in the singular, followed by three specific names). Elsewhere, human beings are enjoined to remember and mention the "Name of God" (singular) in prayer or when slaughtering animals. But as seen in the Qur'anic passages I quoted at the outset, God's names are also mentioned in the plural, and He is referred to by many names in the Qur'an. Even so, the Qur'an offers no definitive list of names for God. There are multiple *ṣaḥīḥ* hadiths in which the Prophet Muhammad asserts that God has ninety-nine names, "100 minus one," and that a great reward will come to those who enumerate (*aḥṣā*) or memorize (*ḥafiẓa*) all of them.[3] Even in the collections of hadith, however, we find no single definitive list of such names. There are two hadiths in the canonical collection of Ibn Majah, for example, that give largely overlapping, but not identical, lists of the ninety-nine names of God; and a quick perusal of such lists in other traditional Muslim sources makes it clear that there is no single, official list of Divine Names. Indeed, the hadiths just cited, indicating the virtue and reward to be had for knowing all of the ninety-nine names of God seems to have spurred Muslims to examine the Qur'an themselves for precisely this purpose. The fact that the various lists are not identical makes it clear that God's self-naming cannot be definitively circumscribed or delimited by human effort. Even the additional clarification in the hadith that God's names are "100 minus one" seems superfluous, unless it is suggesting that there is another name for God that remains a mystery and transcends the boundaries of human knowing—perhaps a name that God keeps to Himself.[4]

In this chapter I present an overview of the various ways in which God is "named" in the Qur᾿an, and the relationship of the Qur᾿anic naming of God to the lists of Divine Names given in the hadith and devotional literature. Then I explore what the purpose of God's many names in the Qur᾿an might be, what it might mean for human beings to "name God"—that is, to make use of His names, and what the Qur᾿an intends human beings to do with these names.

Of course, the most frequently mentioned name for God in the Qur᾿an is Allah, which is sometimes considered an elision of the Arabic "*al-ilāh*," meaning "the God," but is most commonly understood in Islamic tradition as a proper name for God. This name, which is etymologically related to other Semitic words for God, such as "El," is always listed first among the ninety-nine names. It differs from other Qur᾿anic "Divine Names," however, in that it is the only exclusively "proper" name of God. That is, it names Him without "describing" Him as the other names do. "Allah" is both one of God's multiple names and the name that transcends the multiplicity of His names and encompasses it. Metaphorically, the relationship of the name "Allah" to the other names of God is like the relationship of the singular white light to the multiple refractions of this light that one sees as it passes through a prism. As the prism allows one to see the variations of color seamlessly encompassed by the white light, the multiple names of God allow the human being to discern various aspects of God's essence encompassed, without division, in the name "Allah." As important as the name "Allah" is to the Islamic tradition, it does not seem to have originated with the Qur᾿an, as both the Qur᾿an itself and the broader Islamic tradition suggest that this name was already known to the Arabs of Muhammad's time and city. It may have been used to name the overarching creator deity with whom the pagan Arabs "associated" other false gods, for which they are described as "associaters" (*mushrikūn*).[5] In the very first verses of the Qur᾿an that Muhammad receives, he is told to recite "in the Name of your Lord who created," a description that Muhammad would likely have understood as a reference to "Allah."

The only other name used repeatedly in the Qur᾿anic context as a proper name for God is al-Raḥmān (the Compassionate). Although it is descriptive, it is used as a stand-alone name for God over forty times in the Qur᾿an. This name is mentioned in the opening quote in which people are enjoined to "call upon God (Allah) or call upon the Compassionate (al-Raḥmān)," indicating that on a functional level the names could be considered interchangeable. Besides its use in the Qur᾿an itself, there is some evidence that the name al-Raḥmān was used as a proper name of God by the earliest Muslims. In the *sīra* (biographical literature about the Prophet), there are accounts of the pagan Meccans objecting to the Prophet's new religion because it referred to God by the name al-Raḥmān, a name they did not recognize.[6] Reports that the Arabs took exception to references to God as "compassionate" might be intended to offer some off-handed insight into the pre-Islamic Arab conception of God. However, the fact that they objected to this name in particular suggests both that it was frequently invoked by Muhammad and his followers as a proper "name" (rather than just a description) for God and that, unlike "Allah," it was foreign to the Arabs at that time. This does not necessarily mean it was unknown but perhaps that it was known specifically as a foreign name for God (given Jewish and Christian use of cognate terms and descriptions for God).

The other names for God in the Qur'an, as identified by Muslims, are descriptive. Most are words that take either a typical Arabic adjectival form—for example, al-Raḥīm (the Merciful), al-ʿAzīz (the Mighty), or al-Baṣīr (the Seeing)—or an active participle form—for example, al-Khāliq (the Creator), al-Wārith (the Inheritor), al-Nāfiʿ (the Benefactor). Still other names are impersonal concepts, such as al-Ḥaqq (the Reality), al-Salām (Peace), or al-Nūr (Light). A few of the names typically found in lists of the ninety-nine names, such al-Bāsiṭ (the Open-handed), or al-Mumīt (the Bringer of Death), are not found in the Qur'an in those precise forms but rather are active participles derived from verbs describing actions of God in the Qur'an. The most common descriptive name of God in the Qur'an is, by far, al-Raḥīm (the Merciful), which is etymologically related to al-Raḥmān, and appears with it as a pair in the opening invocation of each Qur'anic *sūra* but one. It is also found in over one hundred other Qur'anic verses, usually paired with al-Raḥmān or with one of two other frequently mentioned names in the Qur'an: al-Ghafūr (the Forgiving), and al-ʿAzīz (the Mighty).

Some well-recognized "names" of God (although not found as commonly in lists) are actually Qur'anic phrases that describe God. Many of them use the common term "Lord" (Rabb), which appears by itself in lists of Divine Names, including the one from Ibn Majah's hadith collection, and is used as a reference for God nearly one thousand times in the Qur'an. It is used in phrases that express God's universal majesty: He is "Lord of the Worlds" (Rabb al-ʿālamīn), "Lord of the Heavens and the Earth" (Rabb al-samāwāti wa'l-arḍ), "Lord of the Throne" (Rabb al-ʿarsh), and "Lord of East and West" (Rabb al-mashriq wa'l-maghrib).[7] But at the same time the term is personal and relational: God is, in various places, "my Lord," "your Lord," or "their Lord." In some Meccan verses, the term *Rabb* is used in phrases meant to indicate God's specific relation to the people and city of Mecca: He is "Lord of this House" (the Kaʿba; Q. 106:3) and "Lord of this City" (Mecca; Q. 27:91); and addressing the Meccans in one case, the "Lord of your fathers" (Q. 44:8). In the Qurʾanic Mosaic narratives, the converted sorcerers at Pharaoh's court proclaim their faith in the "Lord of the Worlds, the Lord of Moses and Aaron"—indicating both God's universal lordship and the special relation with the prophets, Moses and Aaron. Other phrases describing God are also sometimes considered to be among His names, for example: Dhu'l-Jalāli wa'l-Ikrām (Possessor of Majesty and Bounty), Arḥam al-rāḥimīn (Most Merciful of the merciful), or Mālik al-mulk (Possessor of Sovereignty). There is a hadith in which the Prophet Muhammad overhears a man invoking God by the series of descriptions that constitute Sūra 112 of the Qurʾan (Sūrat al-Ikhlās), invoking God as: "Allah, the One, the Eternally Sufficient unto Himself (al-Ṣamad), Who begets not nor was begotten, and none is like unto Him." Upon hearing this, the Prophet declared that the man has called God by "His greatest Name."

These various individual "names" of God in the Qurʾan occasionally occur in clusters but more often occur in pairs. Angelika Neuwirth, among others, has theorized that such pairings of Divine Names play a function in the literary structure of some Qurʾanic *sūras*, where they seem to effect a kind of closure to a particular verse or set of verses—marking thematic shifts in some Qurʾanic *sūras*. Taking their cues from the Qurʾan, however, Muslims themselves were primarily concerned with identifying and learning the Divine Names within the Qurʾan as the proper means to call upon God in their prayers and supplications, or as ways of understanding something about their God who transcends all "likenesses." In Islamic theology, these Divine Names (*asmāʾ*) are discussed primarily as God's attributes or qualities (*ṣifāt*)—terms by which He has not only named but described Himself, and thus as terms by which He could be at least partially known, if never comprehended. Muslims recognized that the various names of God present God not just in multiple but in dialectical ways: as both merciful and just, forgiving and judging, transcendent and immanent, near and far, first and last, outward and inward.[8] Just as they recognized a spiritually edifying dialectic in the tone of the Qurʾanic verses themselves—those that inspire fear repeatedly juxtaposed and balanced with those that inspire hope—so too did they understand the names of God as divided into names of Beauty and Majesty. The names of Beauty were those that presented God as merciful, forgiving, solicitous, and protective of His creatures, and near; while the names of Majesty communicated God's overwhelming power, inescapable judgment, and transcendence. Just as a spiritually healthy tension between the verses of "fear" and "hope" worked to keep the believer metaphorically moving forward along the "straight path," the repeated juxtaposition of Divine Names of Majesty and Beauty, sometimes combined in a single verse, could be said to nourish the believer's proper understanding of God. Qur'an 6:165, for example, describes God as both "Swift in retribution" (*Sarīʿ al-ʿiqāb*) and "Forgiving and Merciful" (*Ghafūr, Raḥīm*).

On that note, I would like to turn now to a consideration of what the purpose of the Qur'an's multiple names of God is for its listeners and readers, what precisely should they *do* with these names of God? As I noted, Islamic scholastic theology treated these names primarily as God's qualities and attributes (*ṣifāt*). The Qur'an itself does not use the term *ṣifāt* in connection with God's names or attributes, but it repeatedly condemns those who falsely "describe" God, using the verb "*waṣafa*," from the same root. Naturally, then, Islamic theologians would understand the descriptive names God uses for Himself in the Qur'an as attributes (*ṣifāt*) that are properly ascribed to God. Yet, I think it is significant that the Qur'an refers to these as "names" rather than as "attributes." A name is, of course, a means by which some particular being can be identified and distinguished from others. In some cases, a name might be descriptive, communicating some knowledge about the named, but not usually in a comprehensive manner. Knowing someone's name may be only the beginning getting to know them, for example. Finally, a name is the means by which someone might be called or summoned; in this sense, it can be a means of power over them. All of these meanings and purposes of a "name" can in one way or another be limiting: to distinguish something is to say that it is this and not that; similarly, to know the descriptive name of a thing is to some extent to be able to define it, and so delimit and circumscribe it. To know the name of a being by which that being might be summoned suggests the possibility of having power over it. Clearly, the Qur'an is not suggesting that human beings have the ability to "name" God in ways that would delimit or grant them power over Him.

The Divine Names given in the Qur'an evade any such limitations by sheer virtue of their quantitative multiplicity as well as their multiple modalities. As I have already noted, these names together effect a kind of dialectic understanding of God as both transcendent and immanent; present and responsive, on the one hand, but beyond all human knowledge on the other; the Lord of all the worlds, but also the Lord of the sacred house in Mecca. Some of the names are names of agency and embody actions, while others are impersonal qualities: Truth, Justice, and Light. Taken together, these Qur'anic names for God remind the Qur'an's listeners and readers that God is everywhere and nowhere that they can define or specify. He is all of the qualities and attributes reflected in His Qur'anic names, and yet He eludes the limits of their definition and lies beyond them. The very multiplicity of the names, chiming repetitively and in diverse forms and combinations throughout the Qur'an, is a constant aural reminder that human knowledge of God can never encompass Him. Perhaps most importantly, above all of these names there is the one, transcendent, and ineffable name that offers no description or definition: the name Allah, which can be said to embody all of God's names.

As important as these Qur'anically given names for God became in Islamic theology as a collective means of "knowing" God, the very idea that the names signified qualities by which God could be known (if not rigidly defined) engendered extensive debates: about the relationship of the "names" themselves to the qualities they semantically signified; about the relationship of these various qualities to God's singular essence; about how their eternity (insofar as they are identical with God's essence) could be squared with their relationality to human beings and their temporalization in speech and language; and about what it could mean for a limited human mind to grasp something of God's nature through these names. By "naming God" with various descriptive names, the Qur'an does implicitly suggest these names as keys to understanding something qualitatively and positively about God, but it does not say so explicitly. Various hadith traditions encourage Muslim believers to "count" or "memorize" God's names—verbs that might be taken to suggest quantitative finitude or that the names are something that one might "collect" or compass in knowledge. Yet the Qur'an itself doesn't focus on the possibility or the importance of knowing *all* of God's names, or on the names as a means to certain knowledge about God, but rather on the importance of using these names—*any* of them—as means to call upon God, to praise Him, to worship Him, and to remember Him. In calling upon God by the names He has given to human beings, the Qur'an assures believers that they can know that God is "near" and that He "responds," even if a palpable sense of His nearness or an apprehension of His response eludes them.

In the Qur'an, God's names are not so much a means to "summon" God, to demand things of Him, or to fully comprehend His nature but to be certain of His presence. The multiplicity of God's names may superficially seem to mimic the multiplicity of gods and names that were objects of worship in pre-Islamic Arab religion, or other forms of polytheism. Perhaps there is even some psychological purpose in this—the indulgence of a people used to calling upon many "names" in their ritual life. But more fundamentally, it is an ironic inversion of this pre-Islamic practice: the multiplicity and interchangeability of the Divine Names fall back upon His Oneness—the names revealed to human beings are many, but the Named is one. The names are but so many doors that grant access to His singular presence. Just as the multiplicity of the names captures the psychological proclivity toward polytheism and redirects it toward the One, the repeated, almost meditative invocation of Divine Names in the Qur᾿an is the Qur᾿anic antidote to idolatry. The conceit of the idol is that it can be a specific and material locus of a divine presence that can be compassed by human knowledge and even human sight and touch, fixed in place and immobile. The Divine Names, by contrast, are multiple and diverse, immaterial—made manifest only by the dynamic and relational act of speech (either God's speech in revealing His names, or human speech in uttering them). The Qur᾿an describes places of worship—mosques, synagogues, and churches—not as homes for idols or even as homes for God but rather as sacred places made sacred because God's Name is mentioned in them. Meat is not consecrated by offering it upon or before stone idols but simply by uttering God's Name over it. God is not in a place or a temple, a sacred rock, or a carved idol; rather, He is wherever His names—any of them—are spoken and remembered.

Notes

1. Qur᾿an 2:31. Literally, the Qur᾿anic verse says that God taught Adam "the names—all of them." Muslim exegetes debate what this refers to. Some say that it was only the names of the angels, or the names of Adam's future progeny. Some even considered it as a metaphor for the knowledge of all languages that humans would speak. Some, however, have understood it as a knowledge of the names (and potentially the realities) of all created things.

2. See Qur᾿an 7:70, 12:39, or 53:19 (the latter with specific reference to the names of the three female deities worshipped by the Quraysh, according to the Qur᾿an and Islamic tradition).

3. See, for example, Bukhari, *Ṣaḥīḥ*, h. 2736; or Muslim, *Ṣaḥīḥ*, h. 2677.

4. Indeed, some hadiths reference the idea of "the greatest name of God" (*ism Allāh al-aʿẓam*)—suggesting a name to which only some (and in Sunni hadith, only the Prophet) have access. It is said to be a powerful name, such that whatever is asked of God through this name is certainly granted. Various Muslim esoteric traditions invoke this concept or discuss what this name might be or those who might be said to know it. However, the broader spiritual effect of the concept (at least for those who do not actually know it!) seems to be to deepen the mystery of God's Name and to balance the confidence of believers able to call upon a responsive God by His Name, with a reminder of their human limitations in either knowing His names, or controlling His response to them.

5. See Qur᾿an 6:136, where the Quraysh are accused of dedicating a share of crops and cattle as offerings to God and a share to the "partners" they associate with Him; or Qur᾿an 29:61: "Were you [Muhammad] to ask them [the Quraysh], "Who created the heavens and

the earth and made the sun and the moon subservient?" They would surely say, 'Allah.' How, then, are they perverted?"

6. For example, in drawing up the Treaty of Hudaybiya between the Prophet Muhammad and the Quraysh, the Qurayshi representative refused to allow treaty to be written in the name of "*Allāh, al-Raḥmān al-Raḥīm,*" saying "We are not familiar with this, so write instead, 'In the name of *Allāh.*'" See Ibn Hisham, *a-Sīra al-Nabawiyya*, 4 vols., ed. M. al-Saqā, I. al-Abyārī, and A. H. Shalabī (Qumm: Matba'at al-Mustafawi, 1936), 3:331–32.

7. Rabb al-'ālamīn is used nearly forty times in the Qur'an, including: 1:2, 5:28, and 7:54. Rabb al-samāwāti wa'l-arḍ is also found over a dozen times in the Qur'an, including 13:16, 19:65, 23:86. Rabb al-'arsh is found in Qur'an 21:22. He is also Lord of the Mighty Throne (Rabb al-'arsh al-'aẓīm); see Qur'an 23:86 and 27:26. Rabb al-mashriq wa'l-maghrib is found in Qur'an 26:68, or in Qur'an 55:17, "Lord of the two easts and the two wests" (*Rabb al-mashriqayni wa Rabb al-maghribayn*).

8. For a more extensive discussion of the theological significance and elaboration of the Divine Names and qualities in Muslim tradition, see Yousef Casewit's chapter 7 in this volume.

4

Qur'an and Hadith on Naming God

Selections for Dialogue

Note: The Qur'an passages included in this chapter are according to the HarperOne publication, The Study Quran*—in which the Arabic* Allāh *is translated as God. To facilitate dialogical study, the Divine Names (terms that describe God and have been identified in the tradition as among God's "names") are italicized.*[1]

The Qur'an on God's "Most Beautiful" Names

al-Fātiḥa (1) 1–7

[1]In the Name of *God*, the *Compassionate*, the *Merciful*. [2]Praise be to *God*,
Lord of the worlds, [3]the *Compassionate*, the *Merciful*, [4]*Master of the Day of
Judgment*. [5]Thee we worship and from Thee we seek help. [6]Guide us upon
the straight path, [7]the path of those whom Thou hast blessed, not of those
who incur wrath, nor of those who are astray.

al-Baqara (2) 31–33

[31]And He taught Adam the names, all of them. Then He laid them before
the angels and said, "Tell me the names of these, if you are truthful."
[32]They said, "Glory be to Thee! We have no knowledge save what Thou
hast taught us. Truly Thou art the *Knower*, the *Wise*." [33]He said, "Adam,
tell them their names." And when he had told them their names, He said,
"Did I not say to you that I know the unseen of the heavens and the earth,
and that I know what you disclose and what you once concealed?"

al-A'rāf (7) 180

Unto *God* belong the most beautiful Names; so call Him by them, and leave those who deviate with regard to His Names. Soon shall they be recompensed for that which they used to do.

al-Ḥashr (59) 22–24

[22]He is *God*, other than Whom there is no god, knower of the unseen and the seen. And He is the *Compassionate*, the *Merciful*. [23]He is *God*, Who there is no god but He, the *Sovereign*, the *Holy*, *Peace*, the *Faithful*, the *Protector*, the *Mighty*, the *Compeller*, the *Proud*. Glory be to Him above the partners they ascribe. [24]He is *God*, the *Creator*, the *Maker*, the *Fashioner*; unto Him belong the most beautiful Names. Whatsoever is in the heavens and the earth glorifies Him, and He is the *Mighty*, the *Wise*.

al-Furqān 25:58–63

[58]And trust in the *Living* who dies not, and hymn His praise. And *God* suffices as one aware of the sins of His servants, [59]He Who created the heavens and the earth and whatsoever is between them in six days, then mounted the Throne, the *Compassionate* [is He]. So ask, regarding Him, one who is aware. [60]And when it is said unto them, "Prostrate before the *Compassionate*," they say, "And what is the *Compassionate*? Shall we prostrate before that [to] which you command us?" And it increases them in aversion. [61]Blessed is He Who placed constellations in the sky and placed therein a lamp and a shining moon. [62]And He it is Who made the night and the day successive, for whosoever desires to reflect or desires to be thankful. [63]The servants of the *Compassionate* are those who walk humbly upon the earth, and when the ignorant address them they say, "Peace."

al-Isrā' (17) 107–110

[107]Say, "Believe in it, or believe not." Surely those who were given knowledge before it, when it is recited unto them, fall down prostrate on their faces. [108]And they say, "Glory be to our Lord! The Promise of our Lord is indeed fulfilled." [109]And they fall down on their faces, weeping, and it increases them in humility. [110]Say, "Call upon *God*, or call upon the *Compassionate*. Whichever you call upon, to Him belong the most beautiful Names. And be not loud in your prayer, nor too quiet therein, but seek a way between."

al-Ḥajj (22) 58–65

[58]And as for those who emigrate in the way of *God* and are then slain or die, *God* will surely provide them with a beautiful provision. And truly *God* is the best of providers. [59]He will surely cause them to enter an entrance with which they shall be content. And truly *God* is *Knowing*,

Clement. [60]Thus it is. And whosoever retaliates with the likes of that which
he has suffered, and is then aggressed upon, *God* will surely help him.
Truly *God* is *Pardoning, Forgiving.* [61]That is because *God* makes the night
pass into the day and makes the day pass into the night, and because *God*
is *Hearing, Seeing.* [62]That is because *God* is the *Truth* and what they call
upon apart from Him is false, and because *God* is the *Exalted*, the *Great.*
[63]Hast thou not considered that *God* sends down water from the sky, and
then the earth becomes green? . . . Truly *God* is *Subtle, Aware.* [64]Unto Him
belongs whatsoever is in the heavens and whatsoever is on the earth. And
God is truly the *Self-Sufficient*, the *Praised.* [65]Hast thou not considered that
God has made whatsoever is on the earth subservient unto you—and the
ship sails upon the sea—by His Command? And He maintains the sky lest
it fall upon the earth, save by His leave. Truly *God* is *Kind* and *Merciful*
unto mankind.

al-Baqara (2) 255

[255]*God*, there is no god but He, the *Living*, the *Self-Subsisting*. Neither slumber overtakes Him nor sleep. Unto Him belongs whatsoever is in the heavens and whatsoever is on the earth. Who is there that may intercede with Him save by His leave? He knows that which is before them and that which is behind them. And they encompass nothing of His knowledge, save what He wills. His pedestal embraces the heavens and the earth. Protecting them tires Him not, and He is the *Exalted*, the *Magnificent.*

Ghāfir (40) 1–3

[1]*Ḥā. Mīm.* [2]The revelation of the Book from *Allāh*, the *Mighty*, the
Knower, [3]*Forgiver of sins, Accepter of Repentance, severe in retribution, Possessed of Bounty.* There is no god but He; unto Him is the journey's end.

The Qur'an on False Gods as "Names That You Have Named"

al-Najm (53) 19–23

[19]Have you considered al-Lāt and al-ʿUzzā [20]and Manāt, the third, the
other? [21]Unto you males and unto Him females? [22]This, then, is an unfair
division. [23]They are naught but names that you have named—you and
your fathers—for which *God* has sent down no authority. They follow
naught but conjecture and that which their souls desire, though guidance
has surely come to them from their Lord.

al-Aʿrāf (7) 70–71

[70]They said, "Have you [Hūd] come unto us that we may worship *God*
alone, and leave aside that which our fathers worshipped? Then bring
upon us that wherewith you have threatened us, if you are truthful." [71]He
said, "Defilement and wrath have already come upon you from your Lord.
Do you dispute with me over names that you have named—you and your
fathers—for which *God* has sent down no authority? Then wait! Truly I
am among those waiting along with you."

Yūsuf (12) 39–40

[39][Yūsuf/Joseph]: O my fellow prisoners! Are diverse lords better, or *God*,
the *One*, the *Paramount*? [40]You worship apart from Him naught but names
that you have named—you and your fathers—for which *God* has sent
down no authority. Judgment belongs to *God* alone. He commands that
you worship none but Him. That is the upright religion, but most men
know not.

The Qurʾan on Devotional/Ritual Invocations of God's Name

al-Aʿlā (87) 1, 14–15

[1]Glorify the Name of thy Lord, the Most High. . . . [14]He indeed prospers
who is purified, [15]remembers the Name of his Lord and prays.

al-Baqara (2):114–115

[114]And who does greater wrong than one who bars [entrance to] the
mosques of *God*, lest His Name be remembered therein, and who strives
for their ruin? They are those who should not enter them, save in fear.
Theirs is disgrace in this world, and theirs is a great punishment in the
Hereafter. [115]To *God* belong the East and the West. Wheresoever you turn,
there is the Face of *God*. *God* is *All-Encompassing, Knowing*.

al-Nūr (24) 35–38

[35]*God* is the *Light* of the heavens and the earth. The parable of His light is
a niche wherein is a lamp. The lamp is in a glass. The glass is as a shining
star kindled from a blessed olive tree, neither of the East nor of the West.
Its oil would well-nigh shine forth, even if no fire had touched it. Light
upon light. *God* guides unto His light whomsoever He will, and *God* sets
forth parables for mankind, and *God* is *Knower* of all things. [36][It is] in

houses that *God* has permitted to be raised and wherein His Name is remembered. He is therein glorified, morning and evening, [37]by men whom
neither trade nor buying and selling distract from the remembrance of
God, the performance of prayer, and the giving of alms, fearing a day when
eyes and hearts will be turned about, [38]that *God* may reward them for the
best of that which they have done and increase them from His bounty.
And *God* provides for whomsoever He will without reckoning.

al-Ḥajj (22):34–35, 39–41

[34]For every community We have appointed a rite, that they might mention
the Name of *God* over the four-legged cattle He has provided them. Your
God is one God, so submit unto Him, and give glad tidings to the humble, [35]whose hearts quiver when *God* is mentioned, and who bear patiently
what befalls them, who perform the prayer, and who spend of that which
We have provided them. . . . [39]Permission is granted to those who are
fought against, because they have been wronged—and truly *God* is able to
help them—[40]who were expelled from their homes without right, only for
saying, "Our Lord is *God*." Were it not for *God's* repelling people, some by
means of others, monasteries, churches, synagogues, and mosques wherein
God's Name is mentioned much would have been destroyed. And *God* will
surely help those who help Him—truly *God* is *Strong, Mighty*—[41]who,
were We to establish them upon the earth, would perform the prayer, give
the alms, and enjoin right and forbid wrong. And unto *God* is the end of
all affairs.

al-Anʿām (6):118–121

[118]So eat of that over which the Name of *God* has been invoked, if you are
believers in His signs. [119]What is with you that you eat not that over which
the Name of *God* has been invoked, when He has expounded for you that
which He has forbidden you, unless you are compelled thereto? Indeed,
many lead astray through their own caprices, without any knowledge.
Surely thy Lord is He Who knows best the transgressors. [120]Forsake sin,
both outward and the inward. Surely those who commit sin shall be
recompensed for that which they used to do. [121]And eat not of that over
which the Name of *God* has not been invoked; truly it is iniquity. Indeed,
the satans inspire their friends to dispute with you, and if you obey them,
you are surely idolaters.

Naming and Names of God in the Hadith

Bukhārī, Adab al-mufrad, *#660*

'Uthman said that he heard the Prophet say, "A person who says every morning and evening thirty-three times, 'In the Name of *God*, by whose Name nothing in the earth or the heaven is harmed, and He is the All-Hearing, the All- Knowing' will not be harmed by anything."

Bukhārī, Ṣaḥīḥ, *#2736*

Narrated from Abu Hurayra: God's Messenger said: God has ninety-nine names—one hundred minus one—whoever counts them will enter the Garden.

Muslim, Ṣaḥīḥ, *#2677*

Narrated from Abu Hurayra: God's Prophet said: To God belong ninety-nine names; whoever commits them to memory will enter the Garden. Truly, Allah is the Odd [in number, i.e., He is one, which is an odd number] and He loves the odd number.

Muslim, Dhikr, *#6*

Narrated by Abu Hurayra: The Messenger of God said: God has ninety-nine names—one hundred minus one—for He is the odd [in number] and loves the odd [numbered]. Whoever commits them to memory will enter the Garden. They are:

God
the One (*al-Wāḥid*)
the Eternally Sufficient unto Himself (*al-Ṣamad*)
the First (*al-Awwal*)
the Last (*al-Ākhir*)
the Outward (*al-Ẓāhir*)
the Inward (*al-Bāṭin*)
the Creator (*al-Khāliq*)
the Maker (*al-Bāri'*)
the Fashioner (*al-Muṣawwir*)
the Sovereign (*al-Malik*)
the Real (*al-Ḥaqq*)
Peace (*al-Salām*)
the Faithful (*al-Mu'min*)

the Protector (*al-Muhaymin*)
the Mighty (*al-ʿAzīz*)
the Compeller (*al-Jabbār*)
the Tremendous (*al-Mutakabbir*)
the Compassionate (*al-Raḥmān*)
the Merciful (*al-Raḥīm*)
the Kind (*al-Laṭīf*)
the Aware (*al-Khabīr*)
the Hearing (*al-Samīʿ*)
the Seeing (*al-Baṣīr*)
the Knowing (*al-ʿAlīm*)
the Magnificent (*al-ʿAẓīm*)
the Righteous (*al-Barr*)
the Transcendent (*al-Mutaʿāli*)
the Majestic (*al-Jalīl*)
the Beautiful (*al-Jamīl*)
the Living (*al-Hayy*)
the Self-Subsisting (*al-Qayyūm*)
the Powerful (*al-Qādir*)
the Paramount (*al-Qāhir*)
the Sublime (*al-ʿAlī*)
the Wise (*al-Ḥakīm*)
the Near (*al-Qarīb*)
the Responsive (*al- Mujīb*)
the Rich (*al-Ghanī*)
the Bestower (*al-Wahhāb*)
the Loving (*al-Wadūd*)
the Thankful (*al-Shakūr*)
the Illustrious (*al-Mājid*)
the Patron (*al-Wājid*)
the Governor (*al-Wāli*)
the Guide (*al-Rashīd*)
the Pardoner (*al-ʿAfuww*)
the Forgiving (*al-Ghafūr*)
the Forbearing (*al-Ḥalīm*)
the Generous (*al-Karīm*)
the Relenting (*al-Tawwāb*)
the Lord (*al-Rabb*)
the Glorious (*al-Majīd*)
the Protecting Friend (*al-Walī*)

the Witness (*al-Shahīd*)
the Manifest (*al-Mubīn*)
the Proof (*al-Burhān*)
the Kind (*al-Raʿūf*)
the Merciful (*al-Rahīm*)
the Originator (*al-Mubdiʾ*)
the Restorer (*al-Muʾīd*)
the Resurrector (*al-Bāʿith*)
the Inheritor (*al-Wārith*)
the Strong (*al-Qawiyy*)
the Severe (*al-Shadīd*)
the One Who brings harm (*al-Ḍārr*)
the One Who brings benefit (*al-Nāfiʿ*)
the Abiding (*al-Bāqi*)
the Protector (*al-Wāqi*)
the One Who humbles (*al-Khāfiḍ*)
the One who exalts (*al-Rāfiʿ*)
the Withholder (*al-Qābiḍ*)
the Open-Handed (*al-Bāsiṭ*)
the One who grants honor (*al-Muʿizz*)
the Humiliator (*al-Mudhill*)
the Equitable (*al-Muqsit*)
the Provider (*al-Razzāq*)
the Possessor of Strength (*Dhu'l-Quwwa*)
the Firm (*al-Matīn*)
the Steadfast (*al-Qāʾim*)
the Eternal (*al-Dāʾim*)
the Preserver (*al-Ḥāfiẓ*)
the Guardian (*al-Wakīl*)
the Originator of creation (*al-Fāṭir*)
the Preserver (*al-Ḥāfiẓ*)
the Guardian (*al-Wakīl*)
the Originator of creation (*al-Fāṭir*)
the Hearer (*al-Sāmiʿ*)
the Giver (*al-Muʿṭī*)
the One who gives life (*al-Muḥyi*)
the One who causes death (*al-Mumīt*)
the Preventer (*al-Māniʿ*)
the Gatherer (*al-Jāmiʿ*)
the Guide (*al-Hādi*)

the Sufficient (*al-Kāfī*)
the Eternal (*al-Abad*)
the Knower (*al-ʿĀlim*)
the Truthful (*al-Ṣādiq*)
the Light (*al-Nūr*)
the Giver of light (*al-Munīr*)
the Perfect (*al-Tamm*)
the Eternally Pre-existent (*al-Qadīm*)
the Odd [in number] (*al-Witr*)
the One Alone (*al-Aḥad*)
the Eternally Sufficient unto Himself (*al-Ṣamad*).

He begets not, nor was He begotten. And none is like unto Him.

Zuhayr [one of the narrators of this hadith] said: We heard from more than one of the people of knowledge that the foremost of these names is revealed (*yuftaḥ*) by the saying: "There is no god but *God,* Him alone, without partner. His is the dominion and all praise belongs to Him. In His Hand is goodness and He is powerful over all things. There is no god but *God,* to Him belong the Most Beautiful Names."

Ibn Mājah, Sunan, *#3859*

Narrated by ʿAʾisha: I heard the Messenger of *Allāh* say: "O *Allāh*! I ask You by Your pure, good, and blessed Name, that which is most beloved by You, that which if You are called by it You respond, and if You as asked by it You give, if You are asked for mercy by it You bestow mercy, and if You are asked for relief from distress by it You grant relief." He said that day: "O ʿAʾisha, do you know that *Allāh* has indicated to me the Name which, if He is called by it, He responds?" I said: "O Messenger of *Allāh*, my father and mother be your ransom! Teach it to me." He said: "It is not for you, O ʿAʾisha." So I moved aside and sat for a while, then I got up and kissed his head, then I said: "O Messenger of *Allāh*, teach it to me." He said: "It is not for you to know, O ʿAʾisha, that I should teach it to you. It is not for you to ask for any worldly things by it." So I got up and performed ablution, then I prayed two cycles of prayer, then I said: "O *Allāh*, I call upon You, *Allāh*, and I call upon You, the Compassionate (*al-Raḥmān*), and I call upon You, the Righteous, the Merciful (*al-Barr, al-Raḥīm*), and I call upon You by all Your beautiful Names, those that I know and those that I do not know, that You might forgive me and have mercy on me." The Messenger of God laughed, then he said: "It is among the names by which you called upon [Him]."

Ibn Mājah, Sunan, *#3857*

Narrated by ʿAbdullah ibn Burayda from his father: The Prophet heard a man say: "O *Allāh*! I ask You by virtue of Your being *Allāh*, the One, the Eternally Sufficient unto Himself, Who begets not nor was begotten, and none is like unto Him." The Messenger of *Allāh* said: "He has asked *Allāh* by His Greatest Name, which if He is asked by it He gives, and if He is called by it He responds.'"

Notes

1. Specifically, Quran verses: 1:17; 2:31–33; 6:118–121; 7:70–72, 114–115, 180, 255; 12: 39–40; 17:107–110; 22:58–65, 34–35, 39–41; 24:35–38; 25:58–63; 40:1–3; 53:19–23; 59:22–34; 87:1,14–15 from *The Study Quran* by Seyyed Hossein Nasr, Editor-in-Chief, Caner K. Dagli, Maria Massi Dakake, Joseph E.B. Lumbard, Mohammed Rustom. Copyright(c) 2015 by Seyyed Hossein Nasr. Used by permission of HarperCollins Publishers.

Part Two

Naming God in Theological Discourse

5

What's in a Name?

A Christian Historical Perspective on Naming God

Christoph Schwöbel

It was with great sadness that the Building Bridges Seminar received news of the sudden death, on September 18, 2021, of Professor Christoph Schwöbel (holder of the 1643 Chair in Divinity at University of St. Andrews in Scotland)—a contributor to six seminar convenings, beginning with "Science and Religion" in Istanbul in 2009. He is remembered fondly not only for his consummate skill in enunciating the breadth and depth of the Christian theological tradition but also for the evident care he took to listen carefully to the Islamic tradition and to elaborate his theology in conversation with Muslim interlocutors. During the 2021 online meeting, he was humanly warm, genuinely enthusiastic, and enormously helpful. He died before completing his intended expansion and annotation of his lecture surveying Christian thought on naming God. Presented here, therefore, is a lightly edited transcript of his oral presentation.

I have been asked to give an overview of naming God in the Christian theological and philosophical tradition. In reflecting on this theme, I have subdivided the points I would like to make into eight short sections.

1. What's in a Name?

The practice of naming God—of calling on God in praise, thanksgiving, petition, and lament; of trying to discern God's address to us, God's human creatures; and of speaking and acting in response to this address—is at the heart of religious life in Christianity and Islam. This practice raises many questions which have exercised believers from the beginning, and it confronts us with all the crucial questions that have also exercised philosophical reflection from early on.

What are the criteria for naming God in an appropriate way? In which way do these forms of naming God differ from our ordinary use of language when we speak about created things? Is *God* a proper name, so that it functions like our own proper names in picking out a particular person? Is God identified through a description—like, "who brought you out of Egypt, the land of slavery," in Exodus 22, or "who raised our Lord Jesus from the dead" (Romans 4:24)—pointing to a narrative that uniquely identifies God? Is it appropriate to use a person-relative designation, like "the God of Abraham, Isaac, and Jacob"? Can *God* be used as a title term, like "Mr. President"? Or is God an index word, like "I," or "you," or "he"? Is it possible to use predicates of God that are not uniquely characteristics of God, be they metaphysical or personal?

One presupposition is shared by our respective religious traditions: all forms of naming God must be based on God's self-identification for human creatures; and every attempt to predicate attributes of God must be based on God's self-interpretation. And can this prevenience of divine self-identification and self-interpretation also be captured philosophically? Does it place limits on the way in which God can be used as a concept in philosophical and theological discourse, if *God* is beyond any category?

2. Naming God in Worship and Philosophical and Theological Reflection: Beginnings as Modified Continuations

When the first communities who understood themselves as living in a continuing community of life with their crucified, risen Lord Jesus of Nazareth came together, they celebrated this communion of life with meals in which they shared the message that, in Jesus's life, death, and resurrection, the God of Israel had opted decisively for the salvation of his people—indeed, of the whole world. They used the scriptures of Israel to name God and applied some ways of naming God to Jesus. The naming of God and Jesus did not replace the naming of God in Israel. Rather, it provided the reason for retaining the naming of God in Israel's Bible and expanded it with new applications of some of the crucial names and new identifying descriptions.

Christian faith spread in the pluralistic religious and philosophical environment of the Mediterranean as a missionary faith claiming to be the true philosophy, the true orientation in life. Philosophy at that time was not an academic exercise. Rather, it was concerned with a cure of the soul, offering a way of formation through wisdom and contemplation. The old question of the origin and principle of everything had acquired a new existential dimension. How can I be saved from the transience and constant perishing of all being in relation to the one that transcends all change and is the principle from which all goodness, truth, and beauty flow? The solution of the relation between the Eternal One and the world, or the perishing many, is often sought by offering a system of ontological gradations which could be envisaged both as a chain of mediating beings and as a ladder, which we have to ascend in order to be united in the ultimate *ekstasis* of the mind with the One which is beyond being.

The theology of the early church put all of its theological energy into maintaining a radical distinction between the uncreated Creator, on the one hand, and the world of creatures, on the other. The doctrine of creation-from-nothing and the insistence on the incarnation of the Creator-Logos in Jesus Christ (who is of one essence with God the Father, and of one essence with us) radically reduce the plurality of mediations. Asserting that the Spirit is also of one essence with God the Father implied that, even where we relate to God and name God, our creaturely possibilities are typically bound to the actuality of God relating to us through the Son and in the Spirit. The doctrine of the Trinity offered the solution for the burning problem of how Christians can call on God the Father and on Jesus, and also pray in the Spirit, without either worshipping a created being—that would be idolatry—or worshipping a plurality of gods—that would be pagan polytheism.

3. What Cannot Be Said of God; and What Must Be Said of God

Apophatic theology, the strategy of naming God by denying creaturely attributes of God, has both biblical and philosophical roots. Both traditions come together in the writings of Dionysius, the unknown philosopher-theologian from around the year 500, who seems to suggest—although only indirectly—that he is the same Dionysius who was converted when Paul preached at the Areopagus in Athens, as mentioned in Acts 17:16–34. We know that "Dionysius" is a pseudonym, because Dionysus's writings contain many extracts from later Neoplatonist philosophers—especially Proclus (ca. 410–485). However, through the assumed authorship by one of Paul's associates, Dionysius's writings enjoyed quasi-Apostolic status in the Eastern church and, later, through translations, also in the Latin West—until pseudonymity was proved by the Italian humanist Lorenzo Valla in the fifteenth century.

In his treatise *On the Divine Names*, Dionysius insists, on the one hand, that we can only truly declare the name of God if we follow the revelation of the scriptures, which are inspired by the Holy Spirit. Those names are given in a symbolic revelation. They refer to the superessential essence of God, which surpasses discursive and intuitive ways. On the other hand, God is revealed in this way as the ground of everything in its supernatural fecundity. According to Dionysius, the way in which God is the ground of everything follows a Trinitarian pattern. The ability to name the unattributable and nameless Godhead remains, nevertheless, a fortuitous gift that can only be asked for in prayer.

A similar tension between what is revealed and the fact that *this* what-is-revealed points to negative attributes in God also appears in the work of the Syrian monk John of Damascus (675–744), whose family probably belonged to the Christian officials who were retained at the court of the Umayyad caliphs when Syria was conquered around 630. He was a priest and monk at the monastery of Mar Saba, near Jerusalem. John is normally regarded as the last of the Eastern Fathers. He is, however, also one of the first to offer a systematic exposition of Christian faith—dogmatics—which is constantly focused on the question of what cannot be said of God and what must be said on the basis of God's revelation.

4. Who Is God? And the Question of the Ground of Being

With Thomas Aquinas (1225–1274), we enter the world of high Scholasticism, characterized by the establishment of the universities, the retrieval of large sections of Aristotle's philosophy communicated through Islamic philosophers, and the intense debate between Jewish, Christian, and Muslim philosophers and theologians that led to a unique culture of rich conversation between the religious and philosophical traditions. In the *Summa Contra Gentiles*—his earlier Summa, which was probably written to provide Christian missionaries with the skills of argument to defend the Christian view over against Jewish and Muslim thinkers—Thomas refers to the name of God—which, with the Septuagint, he translates as "He Who Is." To indicate the ontological uniqueness of God, Thomas argues that everything that exists has its being through participation in being. God is the first being—so does not participate in anything and must be characterized by the identity of being and essence or nature.

The name *I Am Who I Am* indicates exactly that God does not participate in anything; rather, everything that exists participates in God. Thomas's *Summa Theologica* is not an apologetic work. Rather, it is intended as an exposition of the Christian faith for ordinands. The point at which he treats the Divine Names (*ST* I, 13) comes as the concluding reflection on the essence of God in Questions 3–12, beginning with simplicity, perfection, and then going on through all the metaphysical attributes of God. After this he discusses the divine operations from knowledge and will, and God's omnipotence—in order to turn, after that, to the Trinity.

Thomas's reflection on the names of God offers a complete survey of ways of naming God, in which the name of God "I Am Who I Am" (Exod. 3:14) offers the ultimate foundation. Of all the ways of naming God in the identity of the existence and essence of God, "Who is" is the most appropriate name of God—because (a) it does not subsume God under any form; (b) it is not restricted through a mode of apprehension; and (c) it signifies pure presence.

5. Speaking of God and God's Communicative Being

A radical attempt to anchor all naming of God in God's speaking is found in Meister Eckhart (roughly, 1260–1328)—the Dominican theologian, philosopher, and mystic who was accused of heresy and whose rehabilitation is attempted today. In the excerpt provided in this volume, Eckhart describes God as pure Trinitarian self-communication, a Word that speaks itself in the Son, in whom all creatures are spoken.

Eckhart interprets the verses from Jeremiah's calling as a prophet—"The Lord stretched out his hand and touched my mouth and said to me: 'Now I have put my words into your mouth'" (Jer. 1:9)—as the work of the Holy Spirit. The Lord stretching out his hand and the placing of God's words in the mouth of the Prophet is what Eckhart interprets as "the kiss of the soul when mouth is joined to mouth, when the Father gives birth to the Son in the soul, and the soul is spoken to." This moment is the eternal "now." As such, there is a "today" in eternity. In this sense, God's going out is God's coming in. The closer I am to God, the more he speaks himself in me.

6. The God of Promise and Grace

Eckhart's radical view that all naming of God must be based on God's speaking in the Son through the Spirit, which constitutes the possibility of naming God, finds many echoes in the theology of the Wittenberg reformer Martin Luther (1483–1546). Theology is, for Luther, the reflection on the relationship between humans (who are guilty of sin and therefore lost) and the justifying and saving God. The primary modes of theology are therefore prayer, meditation, and what Luther calls "the trials and tribulations of faith." The proper name, which God reveals to Moses, is (in Luther's interpretation) "I will be who I will be." (He correctly translates the Hebrew with a future tense.)

God's essence consists in the fact that He is the only being who is His own future. Therefore, humans are encouraged to hold fast to God and to seek no other grounding for their existence. If God's being is *promise*, then God's attributes must be understood as communicative attributes. God is just—not by requiring humans to become just but by making them just through the gift of grace. This logic of communicative giving reveals God's essence as self-giving love in the Persons of Father, Son, and Holy Spirit. Only in this relationship can God be correctly named and spoken of.

In his mature theology, Luther interprets God's creative activity as speaking the creation into being—so that all creatures are part of God's vocabulary, subject to the rules of divine grammar, and drawn into conversation with a Triune Creator. The essence of God must therefore, according to Luther, be understood as an eternal conversation in the Trinity. So he translates the word *logos* (with Erasmus, for example) in "In the beginning was the *Logos*" (John 1:1) not with *ratio* but with *sermo*—with conversation!

7. Ordering the Names and Attributes of God

The Protestant Reformation—which shapes in its political and cultural effects the political landscape of the West until today—led, of course, to a plurality of churches of the Reformation and to the consolidation of the Roman Catholic Church in the Council of Trent. The reformers retained, however, the confessions of faith of the early church as correct interpretations of scripture. The Westminster Confession of Faith (the next item included in this volume for study) was drawn up by 121 Puritan clergyman in 1646. It was adopted by the General Assembly of the Church of Scotland in 1647 and was ratified by the Scottish Parliament the following year. It was ratified in England only in an amended version that took out all of its most critical aspects. It remains until today a subordinate standard of doctrine—subordinate to scripture as the rule of faith and life—and a primary reference document for all churches in the Calvinist Reformed tradition.

The dogmatic works of the Reformation period offer a detailed scheme of distinctions to order the ways of naming God—listing first the names of God in scripture (which they call *onomatology*) and then distinguishing (in the *pragmatology*) God's absolute "absolutes"—perfection, unity, truth, goodness, independence, eternity, immensity, incomprehensibility, and so on—from the attributes that refer to God's operations and that must therefore be understood as relative or relational attributes (or the "Omni-" attributes).[1]

8. Naming God after the Death of God: Modern and Postmodern Thought Challenges

Almost the whole of nineteenth- and twentieth-century theology and philosophy is concerned with responding to the critique of the European enlightenment: that (a) reference to God can serve as an explanatory factor neither in scientific explanations nor in the understanding of history; (b) the discourse of God transcends the capacities of human knowledge; and (c) it cannot offer a groundwork for moral obligation. For these, the image of the "death of God" put forth by Friedrich Nietzsche (1844–1900) provides the root metaphor for a situation where naming God is no longer part of the unquestionably accepted texture of culture in its different spheres of politics, the economy, institutions for the acquisition of knowledge, and the arts. We can perhaps say that the concept of God has lost its function as the common basis for society, which has created a new space for naming God religiously. That is, the cultural function is lost, but there are new opportunities for the religious ways of naming God.

Postmodernism has brought about a cultural sea change. The strictures of the Enlightenment with regard to the usefulness of the understanding of God are no longer tacitly accepted. The ugly, broad ditch between modernity and what came before it has been breached in many ways. This has made the engagement with traditions that the Enlightenment regarded as obsolete to be the main points of interest for philosophy and theology today.

While there is a functional secularization in many areas of society, the predictions of a substantive secularization as a global and irreversible trend have been met with a situation of radical religious and philosophical pluralism characterized by the revitalization of the historic religions, the emergence of many forms of combinatory spiritualities, and the rise of explicitly antireligious movements. Today there is no aspect of our global situation that can be understood without understanding the role of the religions and their ways of naming God as well as the ways in which the naming of God in any context is contested. This situation presents us with a dialogical imperative to clarify our ways of naming God in conversation. This dialogical imperative implies an invitation to exercise hospitality—intellectual as well as practical—to those whose ways of naming God may differ from ours. Institutions like the Building Bridges Seminar have a very important role to play in meeting these two requirements.

Note

1. Omniscience, Omnipotence, Omnipresence, and (in some lists) Omnibenevolence.

6

Christian Theological Discourse on Naming God

Selections for Dialogue

Pseudo-Dionysius the Areopagite (late fifth/early sixth century)

On the Divine Names

Chapter 1

Dionysius the Presbyter, to his fellow-Presbyter Timothy.

What is the purpose of the discourse, and what the tradition concerning the Divine Names.

1. Now, Blessed Timothy, the *Outlines of Divinity* being ended, I will proceed, so far as in me lies, to an Exposition of the Divine Names. And here also let us set before our minds the scriptural rule that in speaking about God we should declare the Truth, not with enticing words of man's wisdom, but in demonstration of the power which the Spirit stirred up in the Sacred Writers, whereby, in a manner surpassing speech and knowledge, we embrace those truths which, in like manner, surpass them, in that Union which exceeds our faculty, and exercise of discursive, and of intuitive reason. We must not then dare to speak, or indeed to form any conception, of the hidden super-essential Godhead, except those things that are revealed to us from the Holy Scriptures. . . . Yea, it is an Unity which is the unifying Source of all unity and a Super-Essential Essence, a Mind beyond the reach of mind and a Word beyond utterance, eluding Discourse, Intuition, Name, and every kind of being. . . .

4. These mysteries we learn from the Divine Scriptures, and thou wilt find that in well-nigh all the utterances of the Sacred Writers the Divine Names

refer in a Symbolical Revelation to Its beneficent Emanations. . . . And It is called the Trinity because Its supernatural fecundity is revealed in a Threefold Personality, wherefrom all Fatherhood in heaven and on earth exists and draws Its name. And It is called the Universal Cause since all things came into being through Its bounty, whence all being springs; and It is called Wise and Fair because all things which keep their own nature uncorrupted are full of all Divine harmony and holy Beauty; and especially It is called Benevolent because, in one of Its Persons, It verily and wholly shared in our human lot, calling unto Itself and uplifting the low estate of man, wherefrom, in an ineffable manner, the simple Being of Jesus assumed a compound state, and the Eternal hath taken a temporal existence, and He who supernaturally transcends all the order of all the natural world was born in our Human Nature without any change or confusion of His ultimate properties. . . .

7. Thus, then, the Universal and Transcendent Cause must both be nameless and also possess the names of all things in order that It may truly be an universal Dominion, the Centre of creation on which all things depend, as on their Cause and Origin and Goal; and that, according to the Scriptures, It may be all in all, and may be truly called the Creator of the world, originating and perfecting and maintaining all things; their Defence and Dwelling, and the Attractive Force that draws them: and all this in one single, ceaseless, and transcendent act. For the Nameless Goodness is not only the cause of cohesion or life or perfection in such wise as to derive Its Name from this or that providential activity alone; nay, rather does It contain all things beforehand within Itself, after a simple and uncircumscribed manner through the perfect excellence of Its one and all-creative Providence, and thus we draw from the whole creation Its appropriate praises and Its Names. . . . And for myself I pray God grant me worthily to declare the beneficent and manifold Names of the Unutterable and Nameless Godhead, and that He do not take away the word of Truth out of my mouth.[1]

John of Damascus (ca. 674/675–749)

An Exposition of the Orthodox Faith, Book One

Chapter 1

That the Deity is incomprehensible, and that we ought not to pry into and meddle with the things which have not been delivered to us by the holy Prophets, and Apostles, and Evangelists.

No one hath seen God at any time; the Only-begotten Son, which is in the bosom of the Father, He hath declared Him. The Deity, therefore, is ineffable and incomprehensible. For no one knoweth the Father, save the Son, nor the Son, save the Father. And the Holy Spirit, too, so knows the things of God as the spirit of the man knows the things that are in him. Moreover, after the first and blessed nature no one, not of men only, but even of supramundane powers, and the Cherubim, I say, and Seraphim themselves, has ever known God, save he to whom He revealed Himself. God, however, did not leave us in absolute ignorance. For the knowledge of God's existence has been implanted by Him in all by nature. This creation, too, and its maintenance, and its government, proclaim the majesty of the Divine nature. Moreover, by the Law and the Prophets in former times and afterwards by His Only-begotten Son, our Lord and God and Saviour Jesus Christ, He disclosed to us the knowledge of Himself as that was possible for us. All things, therefore, that have been delivered to us by Law and Prophets and Apostles and Evangelists we receive, and know, and honour, seeking for nothing beyond these. For God, being good, is the cause of all good, subject neither to envy nor to any passion. For envy is far removed from the Divine nature, which is both passionless and only good. As knowing all things, therefore, and providing for what is profitable for each, He revealed that which it was to our profit to know; but what we were unable to bear He kept secret. With these things let us be satisfied, and let us abide by them, not removing everlasting boundaries, nor overpassing the divine tradition.[2]

Thomas Aquinas (1225–1274)

Summa contra Gentiles, Book One

Chapter 22

Every thing. . . exists because it has being. A thing whose essence is not its being, consequently, is not through its essence but by participation in something, namely, being itself. But that which is through participation in something cannot be the first being, because prior to it is the being in which it participates in order to be. But God is the first being, with nothing prior to Him. His essence is, therefore, His being. This sublime truth Moses was taught by our Lord. When Moses asked our Lord: "If the children of Israel say to me: what is His name? What shall I say to them?" The Lord replied: "I AM WHO I AM. . . . You shall say to the children of Israel: HE WHO IS has sent me to you" (Exod. 3:13, 14). By this our Lord showed that His own proper name is HE WHO IS. Now, names have been devised to signify the natures or essences of things. It remains, then, that the Divine being is God's essence or nature.[3]

Thomas Aquinas

Summa Theologiae (1260–1328), I, q.13, a. 11

On the contrary, it is written that when Moses asked, "If they should say to me, What is His name? what shall I say to them?," the Lord answered him, "Thus shalt thou say to them, HE WHO IS hath sent me to you" (Exod. 3:13, 14). Therefore this name HE WHO IS most properly belongs to God. I answer that, This name HE WHO IS is most properly applied to God, for three reasons: First, because of its signification. For it does not signify form, but simply existence itself. Hence since the existence of God is His essence itself, which can be said of no other (q 3, a4), it is clear that among other names this one specially denominates God, for everything is denominated by its form. Secondly, on account of its universality. For all other names are either less universal, or, if convertible with it, add something above it at least in idea; hence in a certain way they inform and determine it. Now our intellect cannot know the essence of God itself in this life and, as it is in itself, but whatever mode it applies in determining what it understands about God, it falls short of the mode of what God is in Himself. Therefore, the less determinate the names are, and the more universal and absolute they are, the more properly they are applied to God. Hence John of Damascus says (De Fide Orth. 1), that "HE WHO IS, is the principal of all names applied to God; for comprehending all in itself, it contains existence itself as an infinite and indeterminate sea of substance." Now by any other name some mode of substance is determined, whereas this name HE WHO IS, determines no mode of being, but is indeterminate to all; and therefore it denominates the "infinite sea of substance." Thirdly, from its consignification, for it signifies present existence: and this above all properly applies to God, whose existence knows not past or future, as Augustine says (De Trin. V).[4]

Meister Eckhart (ca. 1260–ca. 1328)

Sermon on Jeremiah 1:9, 10

Augustine says: "the whole of Scripture is in vain. If it is said that God is a word, then he is spoken, but if it is said that God is unspoken, then he is ineffable." But God is something, yet who can speak this word? No one can but he who is the word. God is a word which speaks itself. Wherever he is, he speaks this word, and where he is not he does not speak it. God is both spoken and unspoken. The Father is speaking work, and the Son is working speech. What is in me, goes out of me: if I think something, then my speech reveals it and yet remains within. In the same way the Father speaks the Son who remains unspoken and remains in him. I have said this repeatedly: God's going out is his coming in. The closer I am to God, the more he speaks himself in me.

David says: "The Lord is his name" (Ps. 84:4). "Lord" means the setting up of a supremacy here, while "servant" is a form of subjection. Certain names are proper to God, such as "God," and are detached from all other things. "God" is his truest name, just as "being human" is our name. . . . Certain names signify properties which are attributed to God, such as "son" and "father." When we think of a father, we think simultaneously of a son. There cannot be a father without a son, nor a son without a father, but both contain within themselves an eternal essence which is beyond time. Thirdly, certain names signify both a looking up to God and a turning towards time. God has many names in Scripture. But I say that if someone perceives something in God and gives it a name, then that is not God. God is above names and nature. . . . There is no name we can devise for God. But some names are permitted to us, with which the saints have addressed him and which God has consecrated in their hearts and bathed in a divine light. . . .

The Father speaks the Son with the whole of his power and speaks all things in him. All creatures are the utterance of God. If my mouth speaks and declares God, so too does the being of a stone, and we understand more by works than by words. . . . All creatures wish to echo God in all their works, but they can reveal him only a little. . . . Therefore the Father always speaks the Son in unity and pours forth all creatures in him. They all clamor to return to that place from which they emerged. Their whole life and being is a clamoring and hastening back to him from whom they were born.[5]

Martin Luther (1486–1546)

Sermon on Exodus 3:14

Through this word, He [God] draws all humans from that which is not God, when He says "I am" or "I will be." No creature can say "I am" or "I will be," but only "I perish." A creature does not have essence, which does not change but endures forever. There he has drawn our eyes from all creatures by saying "I will be": By pure faith cling to me, everything else is nothing."[6]

Westminster Confession of Faith (1646)

Article II. Of God, and of the Holy Trinity

I. There is but one only living and true God, who is infinite in being and perfection, a most pure spirit, invisible, without body, parts, or passions, immutable, immense, eternal, incomprehensible, almighty, most wise, most holy, most free, most absolute, working all things according to the counsel of his own immutable and most righteous will, for his own glory; most loving, gracious, merciful, long-suffering, abundant in goodness and truth, forgiving iniquity, transgression, and sin; the rewarder of them that diligently seek him; and withal most just and terrible in his judgments; hating all sin, and who will by no means clear the guilty.

II. God hath all life, glory, goodness, blessedness, in and of himself; and is alone in and unto himself all-sufficient, not standing in need of any creatures which he hath made, nor deriving any glory from them, but only manifesting his own glory, in, by, unto, and upon them: he is the alone fountain of all being, of whom, through whom, and to whom, are all things; and hath most sovereign dominion over them, to do by them, for them, or upon them, whatsoever himself pleaseth. In his sight all things are open and manifest; his knowledge is infinite, infallible, and independent upon the creature, so as nothing is to him contingent or uncertain. He is most holy in all his counsels, in all his works, and in all his commands. To him is due from angels and men, and every other creature, whatsoever worship, service, or obedience, he is pleased to require of them.

III. In the unity of the Godhead there be three persons, of one substance, power, and eternity; God the Father, God the Son, and God the Holy Ghost. The Father is of none, neither begotten nor proceeding; the Son is eternally begotten of the Father; the Holy Ghost eternally proceeding from the Father and the Son.[7]

Notes

1. C. E. Rolt, trans., *Pseudo-Dionysius the Areopagite on the Divine Names and the Mystical Theology* (London: Society for Promoting Christian Knowledge, 1920), 51, 53, 56, 62–64.

2. From E. W. Watson and L. Pullan, trans., *Nicene and Post-Nicene Fathers*, Second Series, vol. 9, ed. by Philip Schaff and Henry Wace (Buffalo, NY: Christian Literature, 1899), rev. and ed. for New Advent by Kevin Knight.

3. Saint Thomas Aquinas, *Summa contra Gentiles, Book One: God*, trans. Anton C. Pegis (New York: Hanover House, 1955). See also Joseph Rickaby, SJ, *Of God and His Creatures: An Annotated Translation (with some abridgement) of the Summa Contra Gentiles of St. Thomas Aquinas* (London: Burns and Oates, 1905).

4. Thomas Aquinas, *Summa Theologica*, trans. by Fathers of the English Dominican, https://www.documentacatholicaomnia.eu/03d/1225-1274,_Thomas_Aquinas,_Summa_Theologiae_%5B1%5D,_EN.pdf.

5. "Sermon 5" (DW 53m W 22) on Jeremiah 1:9, 10, in Meister Eckhart, *Selected Writings*, trans. Oliver Davies (London: Penguin, 1994), 127–30. Reprinted with the kind permission of the translator.

6. Reihenpredigten über 2 Mose, 1524/27 [in] *D. Martin Luthers Werke: kritische Gesamtausgabe* [also called *Weimarer Ausgabe*] 16, 49, 1–4.12. Translation provided by a member of the Seminar.

7. The Westminster Confession of Faith agreed upon by the Assembly of Divines at Westminster, with the assistance of Commissioners from the Church of Scotland, as a part of the covenanted uniformity in religion betwixt the Churches of Christ in the Kingdoms of Scotland, England, and Ireland. Approved by the General Assembly 1647, and ratified and established by Acts of Parliament 1649 and 1690, as the publick and avowed confession of the Church of Scotland, with proofs from the Scripture.

7

Commentaries on the Divine Names

Two Exemplars from the Islamic Tradition

Yousef Casewit

Commentaries on the Divine Names represent a sizable tradition in Islamic thought, as evinced by the existence of more than 150 works in this genre. Broadly speaking, the Divine Names tradition features three major interpretive vectors: the philological, the theological, and the Sufi/mystical. The first vector is exemplified in philological commentaries (*shurūḥ lughawiyya*), such as *Sha'n al-Du'ā'* (Matters concerning supplication) penned by the Shāfi'ī scholar al-Khaṭṭābī (d. 388/998). Such works are predominantly lexicographic exercises in uncovering the variety of meanings of each Divine Name. They function as precursors to the second vector seen in theological texts, such as the classic by al-Bayhaqī (d. 458/1065), *al-Asmā' wa-l-Ṣifāt* (The names and attributes), or al-Juwaynī's seminal theological text, *Kitāb al-irshād ilā qawāṭi' al-adilla fī uṣūl al-i'tiqā* (*The Guide to Conclusive Proofs for the Principles of Belief*), a portion of which is provided in the present volume (see chapter 8). Al-Juwaynī's work takes the earlier philological discussions as its starting point and explicates the meanings of the names within the framework of Ash'arī theology. Such theological commentaries, moreover, were often penned by Sufi-inclined theologians. These authors were attentive to the fact that analyzing the ultimacy of God's names and attributes also generates an awareness of His intimacy. Thus, al-Qushayrī and al-Ghazālī, in his wake, exemplify the third vector in bringing their expertise in Sufism to bear upon the Divine Names tradition. In what follows, I offer a comparative analysis of two important commentators: Abū Ḥāmid al-Ghazālī (d. 1111) and 'Afīf al-Dīn al-Tilimsānī (d. 1291).[1]

Al-Ghazālī

In setting out to expound on a virtue-ethical theory of the Divine Names, the *Maqṣad al-asnā fī sharḥ asmāʾ Allāh al-ḥusnā* (The highest aim in explaining the meanings of God's most beautiful names), in effect, amounts to a sustained theological meditation upon one of the most fundamental paradoxes of monotheism: how to locate and affirm both divine incomparability (*tanzīh*) and comparability (*tashbīh*). To avoid any semblance of theological immanentism, or "the affirmation of God's comparability" (*tashbīh*), al-Ghazālī begins by positing that an unbridgeable chasm, or irreducible "disparity" (*tafāwut*), separates the Lord from the servant. This chasm accounts for a disconnect not only between God's unqualified Essence and the human being but also between the transcendent meanings (*maʿānī*) that reside in the Essence and our limited apprehension of those transcendent meanings in the mind. At the same time, he insists that this chasm does not annul the ethical relevance and ontological reality of the attributes (*taʿṭīl*). Rather, the latter are somehow comparable (*tashbīh*) and serve as prototype for human ethical conduct.

Al-Ghazālī thus grounds his treatise in Ashʿarī voluntarist theology and Sufi virtue ethics and moral psychology. However, there is a palpable theological tension in his cautious use of diction, a hyper-systematized approach to interpreting the Divine Names, and a staunch commitment to a set of semantic and hermeneutical principles that undergird his ethical project and create a space for it to operate within the boundaries of Ashʿarī theological orthodoxy. These principles include his semantic theory of nonsynonymity of the Divine Names, an Avicennan-inspired notion of their transcendent meanings (sing. *maʿnā*), and Ashʿarī volitionism.

The central concern of the *Maqṣad* is expressed in its title: *al-Maqṣad al-asnā fī sharḥ maʿānī al-asmāʾ Allāh al-husnā* (The highest aim in explaining the meanings of God's most beautiful names). The key term here is *maʿnā* (pl. *maʿānī*), whose significance is evidenced by my lack of translation. It is often glossed as pure, transcendent, or suprasensory meaning; concepts that describe it in contrast to a tangible or intelligible "form" (*ṣūra*). At the most basic level, a *maʿnā*, or "meaning," refers to a thing that one intends to convey primarily through language. But the Arabic word that comes closest to this sense of the term *maʿnā* is *al-murād*, or "what is intended" by the speaker. In contrast to the speaker's intended meaning (*al-murād*), the *maʿnā* exists within an individual entity (*fī l-aʿyān*). If it pertains to the sensory realm, then the *maʿnā* of Zayd, for instance, inheres in Zayd. If it pertains to the intelligible realm, then it exists in the mind: my concept of Zayd has a *maʿnā* in my mind *(fī l-dhihn)*.

The chasm between the divine *maʿnā* in the Essence and human apprehension is usually described in the *Maqṣad* as one that is absolute. Although knowledge of the meanings of the Divine Names is inferred from observing that this world necessitates a Creator who possesses essential attributes of life, knowledge, will, and power, these attributes that we grasp from empirical observation only hint at, yet do not truly correspond to God's actual qualities. Unless one is God, one cannot fully know Him, for there is no correspondence between God and other-than-God. Therefore, only God knows God.

In theological terms, what al-Ghazālī means by *maʿnā* of a Divine Name is a unique, inexpressible, inaccessible, inexhaustible, unqualified, and eternal reality, trait, or attribute of God's Essence. Each Divine Name has a *maʿnā* to which it corresponds, which is to say that it has a reality within the unqualified Essence of God. These *maʿānī* are distinctions not divisions, differences not separations, *in divinis.* They are unique to God in their fullness and perfection. Being supraformal, suprasensory, they are not observable and cannot be comprehended by the human intellect. The *maʿnā* of the Divine Name in the human mind is incommensurably limited in relation to the *maʿnā* of that name in the Essence.

Why are the *maʿānī* inexhaustible and incomprehensible? A name like the Determiner (*al-Ḥakam*) or the Equitable (*al-ʿAdl*) would exhaust all human knowledge to be thoroughly explained. The reality of the name the Creator is only known by the one who knows the reality of divine acts (*afʿāl*). This name of act can be known in summary (*bi-l-jumla*) not in detail (*bi-l-tafṣīl*) and not in an exhaustive manner (*bi-l-ḥaṣr*). Due to their incommensurability, al-Ghazālī endorses the Ashʿarī position that our knowledge of the Divine Names is conditional upon revelation. They cannot be rationally inferred, and we must call God by what He calls Himself (*tawqīf*) in scripture. For by naming God on the basis of reason, the caller inevitably commits *tashbīh* by projecting human states and anthropomorphic assumptions onto Him.

Al-Ghazālī insists that the human being can potentially reach a "share" (*ḥaẓẓ*) in all the Divine Names. This human "share" (*ḥaẓẓ*) goes beyond "hearing" the name, for even the eardrum of a dumb beast can capture soundwaves. It also surpasses comprehension of the linguistic meaning of a name, for any simple Arab Bedouin understands the surface meanings of the ninety-nine names. This "share," moreover, surpasses abstract belief in the heart, for any common believer or child has abstract belief. Common believers and exoteric scholars (*ʿulamāʾ*) tend to know the names merely at the level of the uttered sound (*lafẓ*), philological meaning (*lugha*), and abstract belief in the heart.

The servant, he argues, experiences three stages of grace, or "shares" (sing. *ḥaẓẓ*) in the names in progressive stages as he increases in self-knowledge. The first is to cross from abstract belief in a name to concrete certitude of it. For instance, a servant may understand God's power by experiencing his own utter helplessness. The name the Powerful thus becomes immediately evident through "demonstrative unveiling" (*inkishāf burhānī*). This demonstrative unveiling gives rise to an ineluctable certainty and an irresistible attraction toward the beautiful names, provided that the heart is purified of worldly attachments. Finally, the name's magnetic appeal draws the servant to a state of proximity (*qurb*) to the angels and culminates in the bewildering realization that only God actually knows God, and that the servant knows His Lord only insofar as he knows himself. Note that al-Ghazālī intentionally privileges the servant's proximity to an angelic ideal. He does not hold God as such, nor Adam's primordial perfection (*kamāl ādamī*, as Ibn ʿArabī would put it), as the human ethical ideal.

For al-Ghazālī, knowledge of God and the process of characterizing oneself by God's character traits (*takhalluq*) culminates in a bewildering state of dismay (*dahsha*, *ḥayra*) that we are incapable (*ʿajz*) of truly knowing God, and a certitude that God in Himself cannot be realized. This state of bewilderment captures the simultaneous affirmation and negation of the possibility of knowing God, and it goes hand in hand with the process of discovering the names. For just as the *maʿānī* face two directions (the Essence and the names), the servant faces two infinitudes: there is no end to what we *can* know about God, just as there is no end to what we *cannot* know about God.

The names thus both veil and reveal God's perfection, and although none of the Divine Names and attributes can be fully known, exhausted, or reduced to meaningless proper nouns, the more one begins to grasp the perfection of the meanings of the Divine Names, the more one comprehends how short one has fallen. The furthest goal (*ghāya*) and highest aim of al-Ghazālī's *Maqṣad* is to offer intimations (*īmāʾ*) of the keys to unlocking this state of bewilderment by offering synoptic insights into the core creedal beliefs concerning the names.

Al-Tilimsānī

Many Sufis have responded to the apparent contradictions and theological tensions pointed out by al-Ghazālī by evoking the servant's annihilation in (*fanāʾ*) and subsistence through (*baqāʾ*) the Lord, thereby collapsing the servant/Lord binary. Al-Ghazālī, as a Sufi theologian with a broad readership, refuses to blur those lines. Al-Tilimsānī has no hesitations in doing so.

The core difference between commentaries on the Divine Names written by proponents of the Akbarī tradition, on the one hand, and Sufi-Ashʿarī commentators such as al-Qushayrī and al-Ghazālī, on the other, is that the former take to heart the proclamation that only God is real, and that the realm of other-than-God is ultimately unreal. In fact, al-Tilimsānī's mystical theology is not only guided by this foundational tenet; it brazenly takes it to its ultimate conclusions.

Although the Ashʿarī-Sufi commentators tend to make nondualist proclamations in their writings too, they tend to wear many hats and to work out their theology within dualist binaries of God and other-than-God posited by the Ashʿarī theological tradition. In contrast, al-Tilimsānī works out a thorough mystical theology with terminological consistency, scriptural faithfulness, and daring profundity.

The contrast between commentaries written by proponents of the Ibn ʿArabī tradition versus those written by Sufi-Ashʿarīs is thrown into sharp relief in passages that discuss the ultimate religious experience of annihilation in God (*fanāʾ*). Sufi-Ashʿarīs like al-Qushayrī, al-Ghazālī, or the Malagan scholar Ibn al-Marʾa (d. 611/1214) inhabit a world that posits a separation between God and other-than-God. For them, the servant's annihilation in God (*fanāʾ*) tends to be described as a passing away in God's will. When the servant perishes, the servant/Lord binary collapses in the sense that only the Lord's will remains. The servant's will becomes aligned with the Lord's to such an extent that it is indistinguishable from the Lord.

According to al-Tilimsānī, this state of passing away in the Lord's will is actually an experience of the fact that all acts ultimately belong to God. It is a witnessing of "the oneness of God's acts" (*tawḥīd al-afʿāl*). Those who witness the oneness of God's acts (*tawḥīd al-afʿāl*) are sustained by His attribute of Self-Subsistence (*qayyūmiyya*). For them, the servant's devotions subsist through God. As such, there is no Speaker other than God, and no Hearer other than Him.[2] As the wayfarer continues to journey in God, his egoic sense of separative existence melts away, and he witnesses the oneness of God's names and qualities (*shuhūd al-asmāʾ waʾl-ṣifāt*). For the acts are derived from the names (*asmāʾ*) and qualities (*ṣifāt*), and when the names and qualities are witnessed, the acts themselves dissolve. At this stage, not only does God act through all agents, but the act of speech itself disappears in the essential quality of divine knowledge.[3] Beyond that, the highest level of witnessing is to pass away in God's Essence, thereby traversing the acts, names, and attributes of God. The witnesser of the divine Essence proclaims the all-inclusive oneness of the Essence (*shuhūd al-dhāt*) and experiences the Unity of the All; that is, that there is nothing else with Him.[4] From the perspective of God's exclusive oneness, all purported actions, qualities, speech, hearing, perfections, and lack thereof belong to Him at various levels of existence and are experienced through the Essence.[5] Direct witnessing (*mushāhada*), as the standard of wayfaring and *maʿrifa*, is not *tafakkur* (meditation). Rather, it is a visual experience of the Light of the Names.

The Root Names

According to al-Tilimsānī, Allāh and al-Raḥmān (the All-Merciful) are the two Root Names (*asmāʾ al-uṣūl*). They serve as the "gathering place" for all the other Names—which are their "branches" (*asmāʾ al-furūʿ*). The Qurʾan states: "Say: Call upon Allāh, or call upon al-Raḥmān; whichever you call upon, His are the most beautiful names" (*Isrāʾ* [17]110). For al-Tilimsānī and the Akbarī tradition in general, this verse alludes to two points of access to the divine Essence, or two modes through which God relates to the realm of other-than-God. Allāh is a name of transcendence that points to the Essence, whereas al-Raḥmān is a name of immanence that points to both the Essence and to its intrinsic quality of mercy and existentiation. Thus, Allāh evokes names and qualities of transcendence, majesty, incomparability, rigor, deprivation, dominance, constriction, death, harm, inaccessibility, nonexistence, and vengeance. Al-Raḥmān, for its part, denotes unconditioned existence, bestowal, beauty, existence, benefit, expansiveness, forgiveness, assistance, life, kindness, and generosity. Al-Tilimsānī's commentary on these two names, which are the first and second entries in the commentary, offer a detailed list of the Branch Names that fall under each Root Name. He explains how some Divine Names are included within the name Allāh because they indicate His otherness. These apophatic names designate God's not-being-what-we-are (*ʿadamī*). They include names of transcendence such as the Exclusively One (Aḥad), or the Compeller (Jabbār). Others are cataphatic names that indicate being, mercy, and a relation between God and man such as the Ever-Merciful (Raḥīm) or the Bountiful (Dhu ʾl-Faḍl).

The dynamic between the names Allāh and al-Raḥmān determines the infinite levels of existence, the structure of the cosmos, and the interpenetration of the Divine Names and their properties and traces in creation. The outpouring of existence from the name al-Raḥmān is thus interrupted by the transcendence of the name Allāh. Hence, the realm of other-than-God comprises existence in a hierarchical and ranked mode. The names included within the name Allāh are "Names of Rank" (*al-asmāʾ al-martabiyya*) because they are responsible for demarcating sheer existence into levels. These names are also called the "Names of Nonexistence" (*al-asmāʾ al-ʿadamiyya*) because they negate the ontological flow of the All-Merciful. Each name is contained within each name. The names are both hierarchical and coequal.

Concluding Thoughts

An ontological turn in the tradition was instigated by Ibn ʿArabī (d. 637/1240) and his students—who engage with the names, not from an Ashʿarī volitionist perspective but as ontological relationships (sing. *nisba*) between God and creation. As a result, occult meditations on the names are absent from Ghazālī's commentary. In contrast, al-Tilimsānī and later commentators tend to include discussions of the talismanic, magical, and healing properties of the names as remedies to ailments in the soul. These remedies, which are acquired by invoking the names, are a common feature of Divine Names commentaries in the later Islamic Middle period.

Moreover, this ontological turn in the Divine Names tradition raises a host of new questions and solves some of the theological anxieties that are so clearly palpable in the *Maqṣad*. Thus, whereas al-Ghazālī treats names like the Ever-Merciful (al-Raḥīm) or the Inflictor of Harm (al-Ḍārr) as aspects of God's will to bless or punish a servant, Ibn ʿArabī and his school prioritize the servant's subjective response to God's singular reality depending on his capacity or "preparedness" (*istiʿdād*) for that encounter. The servant responds to the disclosed properties of these contrary names, displaying "agreeability" (*mulāʾama*), "disagreeability" (*munāfara*), "readiness" (*tahayyuʾ*), or "preparedness" (*istiʿdād*) for the divine self-disclosure. As such, God as "the Inflictor of Harm" is really a manifestation of an unprepared servant's response to His disclosure. Al-Ghazālī briefly evokes the concept of "agreeability" in the *Maqṣad*. However, he prioritizes Ashʿarī definitions of divine mercy and wrath as God's will to bless or punish in order to avoid the implication that God is qualified by imperfect human emotions and psychological states.

Notes

1. Here I have chosen to focus on ʿAfīf al-Dīn al-Tilimsānī (a contemporary of Meister Eckart) because he is a brilliant author and deserves to be better known.
2. Al-Tilimsānī, *In the Names of God*, § 19.2.
3. Al-Tilimsānī, § 92.6.
4. Al-Tilimsānī, § 16.1.
5. Al-Tilimsānī, § 129.3.

8

Muslim Theological Discourse on Naming God

Selections for Dialogue

Imām al-Ḥaramayn al-Juwaynī

A Guide to Conclusive Proofs for the Principles of Belief

(Kitāb al-irshād ilā qawāṭiʿ al-adilla fī uṣūl al-iʿtiqād)

A Statement of the Meaning in the Names of God, the Exalted

Chapter on the Law and the Names of God

Whatever names and attributes the law uses to refer to the Exalted God, we also use; and whatever the law forbids as a reference for God, we likewise forbid. In regard to those for which there is neither explicit authorization nor prohibition, we offer no judgment, neither endorsing nor forbidding them. The rulings of the law derive from the sources of tradition and, if we were to determine an endorsement or a prohibition without legal precedent, we would be affirming the application of a judgment that is outside of tradition.

Still, in regard to allowing the application of a term [to God], we make no stipulation that there be a definitive ruling on it in the law. Rather, it is sufficient that practice necessarily involves it, even though there be no explicit evidence that would make it obligatory. Despite the fact that legal analogies are used in determining the requirements of practice, adherence to such analogies is not permitted in regard to the designation of the Lord and His attributes. Understand well!

Chapter on the Meanings of the Names of God

Our Shaykh, may God be pleased with him, divided the names of the Lord, may He be sanctified and exalted, into three categories:

1. He maintained that among [God's] names are those by which we say that He is He. That is, all those in which the designation for Him indicates His very existence.
2. Others of His names are those by which we mean that He is something other than He. That is to say, all those (names) in which the designation for Him indicates an action, such as the names "The Creator" or "The Sustainer."
3. Yet other names for Him are those by which is meant neither that He is He, nor that He is other than He. This category includes all those names in which the designation indicates an eternal attribute, such as the names "The Knower" (al-ʿĀlim) and "The Powerful" (al-Qādir).

One of our leading masters remarked that each name is the thing named in itself and this led to saying the Lord, may He be sanctified and exalted, when He is called Creator, Creator is the name and it is the Lord God. Creator, however, is not the name for creating, nor is creating the name for the Creator. He further generalized this for all the other categories.

The better approach, in our view, is that of our shaykh. Here the names occupy the position of the attributes. When names are used without entailing a negation, they refer to a positive certainty. Thus, when we say: "God, the Creator," we are obliged to comprehend in that term a positive fact, which is the fact of creation. The meaning of "Creator" is 'the one because of whom there is creation.' But there is no attribute of creation that actually links back to the [divine] essence. The term "Creator" indicates nothing but the affirmation of creation. For that reason our leading masters stated: The Exalted Creator (al-Bārī) cannot be characterized in His [pre-]eternity as being a creator, since there existed no creation in [pre-]eternity. Were He to be described in this way to indicate that He is all-powerful, such usage would only be metaphorical. He distinguished from this "knowledge" and "power," since they are both attributes [of the divine] and are also both names. The discussion concerning this matter has its roots in the dispute about whether to employ a term or whether its use is forbidden.

So all of the names of the Lord are classified according to whether they indicate the Essence or the eternal attributes [categories 1 and 3, above], or whether they rather indicate actions or the negation of those things above which the Exalted Creator is hallowed [category 2, above]. At this point we will provide a brief explanation of the names that are sanctioned by tradition.

As for the name "Allāh," the truth is that it is the equivalent of the proper name of God, may He be sanctified. There is no etymology for it. Nevertheless, some say that its root is *ilah* to which is added a *lām* to enhance the following vowel. Others say *al-ʾilāh* from which they subtract the intermediate *hamza* and assimilate the *lām* for the enhancement of what follows it. Yet others say that its root is *lāh* into which is inserted the *lām* of enhancement. Some lexicographers maintain that it derives from *al-taʾalluh* which is "worshipping." Thus the meaning of Allāh is "the one who is the object of worship."

"Al-Raḥmān al-Raḥīm" [the Merciful, the Compassionate (Q 1:3)] are two names taken from the word *al-raḥma* [mercy]. According to the most competent authorities, they both have the same meaning, much like *al-nadmān* [repentant] and *al-nadīm* [regretful]. Nevertheless, al-Raḥmān designates specifically the Exalted God and cannot be applied to anyone else. Furthermore, *alraḥma* denotes, in the view of the best authorities, the desire of the Exalted God to confer favour on His servant. The two names are among the attributes of essence, although some scholars see in the word *al-raḥma* this very idea of conferring favor and would therefore have "al-Raḥmān al-Raḥīm" belong to the attributes of action.

"Al-Malik" [Sovereign] means the One who possesses sovereignty. But thereafter they disagree as to the meaning of sovereignty. Some explain it as meaning creation, so that the sovereign is the Creator and that is one of the names of action. Others say that sovereignty is the power to originate [*ikhtirāʿ*] since one says "so-and-so possesses (*yamlik*) the advantages of his fortune," meaning thereby he achieves power by means of it. In that way this name is the name of an attribute. The Exalted Lord is always and will always be sovereign. . . .

"Al-Wāsiʿ" [the All-comprising]: It is said to mean "the knowledgeable [*al-ʿālim*]"; others say "the munificent" [*al-jawād*], since one describes the munificent person as having an expansive breast and not being tight-fisted. Yet others say that this term has the sense of the self-sufficient [*al-ghaniy*], but we will explain self-sufficiency further in the section on justice.[1]

Abu Hamid Muhammad al-Ghazālī, (ca. 1056–1111)

The Ninety-Nine Beautiful Names of God

al-Maqṣad al-asnā fī sharḥ asmāʾ Allāh al-ḥusnā

Part One: Chapter Four

On Explaining That a Person's Perfection and Happiness Consists in Being Molded by the Moral Qualities of God

You should know that whoever has no part in the meanings of the names of God—great and glorious—except that he hears the words and understand the linguistic meaning of their explication and their determination, and except that he believes with his heart in the reality of their meanings in God most high—such a one has an ill-fated lot and a lowly rank and ought not boast of what he has achieved. For hearing the words requires only the soundness of the sense of hearing, through which sounds are perceived, and this is a level in which beasts share. As for understanding their determination in language, all one needs is a knowledge of Arabic and this level is shared by those adept in language and even by those Bedouin who are ignorant of it.[2] As for faith affirming their meanings of God—may He be praised and exalted—without any revelatory vision, all one needs to understand the meaning of the words and to have faith in them, and this level is shared by the common people, even by young boys.[3] For once one has understood the teaching, if these meanings were presented to him, he would [i] receive them and memorize them, [ii] believe them in his heart, and [iii] persist in them. These are the levels of most scholars, to say nothing of those who are not scholars. In relation to those who do not share with them in those three levels, these should not be denied credit, yet they are clearly deficient with respect to the acme of perfection. For "the merits of the [merely] pious are demerits of those who have drawn near to God." Indeed those who have drawn near to Him share in the meanings of the names of God the most high in a threefold way.

The first share is a knowledge of these meanings by way of witnessing and unveiling so that their essential realities are clarified for them by a proof which does not permit any error; and God's possession of these meanings as His characteristics is revealed to them in a disclosure equivalent in clarity to the certainty achieved by a mean in regard to his own inner qualities, which he perceives by seeing his inward aspect, not by outward sensation. How great a difference there is between this and a faith derived from one's parents and teachers by conformity and persistence in it, even though it be accompanied by argumentative proofs from Kalām!

A second way of sharing in these meanings belongs to those who so highly esteem what is disclosed to them of the attributes of majesty that their high regard releases a longing to possess this attribute in every way possible to them so that they may grow closer to the Truth—in quality not in place; and with the possession of such characteristics they become similar to the angels, who have been brought near to God—great and glorious. Moreover, it is inconceivable that a heart be filled with high regard for such an attribute and be illuminated by it without a longing for this attribute following upon it as well as a passionate love for that perfection and majesty, intent upon being adorned with that attribute in its totality—inasmuch as that is possible to one who so esteems it. And if not in its totality, the esteem for this attribute will necessarily provoke in him the longing for as much of it as he can assimilate. . . .

The third share follows upon the effort to acquire whatever is possible of those attributes, to imitate them and be adorned with their good qualities, for in this way man becomes "lordly"—that is, close to the Lord most high, and so becomes a companion to the heavenly host [*al-mala' al-a'lā*] of angels, for they are on the carpet of proximity [to God]. Indeed, whoever aims at a likeness to their qualities will attain something of their closeness to the extent that he acquires some of their attributes which bring them closer to the Truth most high. . . .

Part Two: Chapter One

On Explaining the Meanings of God's Ninety-Nine Names

4. Al-Malik—the King—is the one who in His essence and attributes has no need of any existing thing, while every existing thing needs Him. There is nothing among things which can dispense with Him concerning anything—whether in its essence or its attributes, its existence or its survival; but rather each thing's existence is from Him or from something that is from Him. Everything other than He is subject to Him in its essence and its attributes, while He is independent of everything—and this is what it is to be king absolutely.

Counsel: The creature cannot be conceived of as being king absolutely, for he cannot dispense with everything; indeed, he will always be needy with regard to God the most high, and would be even if he were able to dispense with all but Him. Nor can one conceive of a creature having everything in need of him since most existing things have no need of him. But to the extent that it is conceivable for one to be free from some things while other things need him, one may have a taste of kingship.

For a king among people is one whom no one rules but God the most high, and who does not need anything except God—great and glorious. And with that he rules his kingdom insofar as his soldiers and his subjects obey him. Yet the kingdom proper to him is his own heart and soul, where his soldiers are his appetites, his anger, and his affections; while his subjects are his tongue, his eyes, his hands, and the rest of his organs. If he rules them and they do not rule him, and if they obey him and he does not obey them, he will attain the level of a king in this world. And if that be coupled with the fact that he is independent of all people, yet all people are in need of him for their life now and in the future, he will be an earthly king.

This is the level of the prophets—may God's blessings be upon all of them. For they have no need of direction to the next life from anyone except God—great and glorious—while everyone needs it from them. They are followed in this kingship by the religious scholars who "inherit the legacy of the prophet." Their kingship, however, is proportional to their ability to guide the people and to their lack of need for asking for guidance.

By means of these attributes [humankind] comes close to the angels in qualities, and by means of them approaches God the most high. The kingship is a gift to man from the true king whose sovereignty has no competitor.

One of the "knowers" [*ʿārifūn*] was right to respond to a prince who said to him: "Ask me for what you need" by saying: "Is that the way you speak to me when I have two servants who are your masters?" When he said: "Who are these two?" the knower answered: "Greed and desire: for I have conquered them yet they have conquered you; I rule over them while they rule you." And one of them said to a certain shaykh: "Advise me," and he said to him: "Be a king in this world and you will be a king in the next." When he said: "How might I do that?" the shaykh answered: "Renounce this world and you will be a king in the next." He meant: detach your needs and your passions from this world, for kingship lies in being free and able to dispense with everything.[4]

ʿAfīf al-Dīn al-Tilimsānī (d. 690/1291)

In the Names of God: A Mystical Theology of the Divine Names

85. al-Kafīl: The Sponsor

85.1. Both al-Bayhaqī and Abū l-Ḥakam agree that it is a divine name, but not al-Ghazālī. It is cited in the Surah of al-Naḥl in the verse: "you have made God a Sponsor over you" [Q. Naḥl (16):91]. As for God's sponsoring of His servants' provisions, that is through His name the Provider. His bringing them into existence, moreover, is through His name the Creator. The loving kindness that they hope from Him is through His name the Loving Kind. His repelling of harms that they fear is through His names the Protector and the Repeller. Furthermore, *kafīl* means the guarantor, and He gives His sponsored subject "a twofold portion, *kiflayn*, of His mercy" [Q. Ḥadīd (57):28.]. *Kifl* means "double," and hence He "doubles for whomever He wills" [Q. Baqara (2):261].

85.2. The guarantee of all things rests upon His existence. However, He returns the thing by returning its equivalent, not the thing-in-itself, because there is no repetition in existence, and there is no constraint on the breadth of divine munificence. Therefore, He sponsors the return of the night, and the regress of the day after it departs, and wakefulness that returns after sleep, and sleep that returns after wakefulness between night and day. He is the Sponsor of the faculties of motion that come after rest, and of the glances that are successively bestowed upon the eyes. He sponsors the return of what has passed such that the faculty of memory recalls its affairs in this world and the next. He is the agent behind all acts, and the Bestower of sense perception and imagination in that He sponsors the needs of His servants for those faculties. He guarantees that the seeker shall attain what he seeks. And were it not for the confidence in His sponsorship of moments of respite, no soul would entertain any hope for attainment. Wherefore, His sponsorship expands the soul; and were it not for it, the terror of nonexistence would eradicate all intimacy. Were this not so, how could the one in whom nonexistence is intrinsic continue to exist until tomorrow, or how could it even remain steadfast after the passing of yesterday?

85.3. Nonetheless, souls find within themselves the name the Sponsor and they depend on it, placing their hopes in it. This occurs in such a way that the veiled person is unaware of it. As for the witnesser, he sees it with his own eyes, just as the believer affirms it through faith. You eat food and expect to become satiated; and were it not for His sponsorship, you would have no hope. For if you did not behold His guarantee, you would not be content with your fill, and without it you would become covetous. You would never feel secure, and you would always expect the worst. However, souls sense the name the Sponsor, and that inspires them to hope for the best. The more one places confidence in the name the Sponsor, the more one finds serenity in the flow of destiny. This confidence, moreover, is precisely commensurate with the perfection of the soul, and the soul's preparedness is in accordance with it. The soul finds support through the property of the name the Sponsor. Every sponsorship that takes place in which a soul finds confidence is one of the branches of His sponsorship.

85.4. This invocation is very beneficial for those who wish to attain the station of trust in God. And God knows best.

68. al-Mughīth: The Deliverer

68.1. This noble name envelops His existence and mercy. It appears in the Surah of al-Anfāl in the verse: "When you called upon your Lord to deliver you, and He responded to you" [Q. Anfāl (8):9]. It is only through the name Deliverer that the petition of the caller for God's deliverance is granted. Of the three eminent scholars, only al-Bayhaqī affirms that this name is a name of God. The Deliverer is synonymous with the Helper—"help is only from God" [Q. Āl 'Imrān (3):126]—yet it also pertains to the name the Responsive, which is why He said: "and He responded to you."

68.2. Calling for deliverance is an appeal to the Deliverer by way of a supplication to God. It is invoked only during a crisis or a state of hardship—and the cosmic levels of such states are not limited to the meanings in this world and the next. The petitioner may say: "Oh my deliverance!" If he means to address his Lord, then he actually means "Oh Deliverer!" However, if he means to address some creature, then what he means is mistaken with respect to his intent, although in actual reality it is also correct since there is no deliverance except God's. Besides, there is none but He, regardless of whether the petitioner for deliverance knows this or not.

68.3. When the petitioner calls for deliverance from a crisis of hunger, then he is appealing to the name Deliverer insofar as it shares in the meaning of the name Provider. When he calls for deliverance from a crisis of poverty, then he is beseeching the Deliverer insofar as it shares in the meaning of the name the Enricher—and the variation in types of enrichment is unlimited. When he calls for deliverance from a crisis of abasement, then he is calling upon the name Deliverer insofar as it partakes in the name Exalter. In summary, the names interpenetrate and their meanings differentiate with respect to the passive recipients and the active agents involved.

68.4. The presence of the name Deliverer also reciprocates the demands of each person's state. For the nonverbal language of spiritual states does not err, while verbal language may err. When the petitioner calls for deliverance from a crisis of religion, then he is imploring the name the Deliverer from the presence of the name the Guide. He receives deliverance from the Deliverer in accordance with the dictates of his state at its specific stage of guidance. Moreover, all crises of religion ensue from the presence of the name Misguider in the stages of worship, Sufism, direct recognition, halting beyond all stations, and separation, but there is no misguidance at the level of the axial Pole when it is truly attained—that is, the end of the Second Journey. Likewise, there is no misguidance in the two final Journeys.

68.5. It is not possible for someone to call for deliverance without being delivered either outwardly or inwardly. However, if he does not receive deliverance from the levels of worldly crises, then he is compensated in the levels of the hereafter. The least of his degrees of deliverance is his own inward impulse to call upon deliverance, which is a quality of perfection that awakens in the soul. The soul thereby seeks to avail itself from the slumber of heedlessness caused by hankering after spiritual states and bodily and financial well-being, and by a soul that is submerged in desolate darkness. Moreover, whoever calls upon God for deliverance but fails to recognize its outward form should know that his persistence in petitioning is an aspect of the deliverance of the Maker. For the state of petitioning is itself a cause of nearness to God.

68.6. Invoking this name during the spiritual retreat benefits the one who is in a state of dispersion and hardness of the heart, for it removes them. And God knows best.[5]

Notes

1. Imām al-ḥaramayn Al-Juwaynī, *A Guide to Conclusive Proofs for the Principles of Belief* (*Kitāb al-irshād ilā qawāṭiʿ al-adilla fī uṣūl al-iʿtiqād*), trans. Paul Walker (Reading, UK: Garnet, 2000), 78–91, amended slightly. Reprinted with permission from the Muhammad

Bin Hamad Al-Thani Center for Muslim Contribution to Civilization at Hamad Bin Khalifa University (Doha, Qatar).

2. The Bedouin reference is two-edged since their traditional way of life, rooted in early Arabic verse and linguistic habits, made them a repository of the language of the Qurʾan, however unlettered they may have been.

3. Richard McCarthy renders *al-mushāhada* (direct witnessing) and *al-mukāshafa* (unveiling) as "revelation" and "direct vision." Ghazālī contrasts these ways of knowing to that of mere conformity to observants (*taqlid*).

4. Abu Hamid Muhammad al-Ghazālī, *The Ninety-Nine Beautiful Names of God* (*Al-Maqṣad al-asnā fī sharḥ asmāʾ Allāh al-ḥusnā*), trans. David Burrell and Nazih Daher (Cambridge: Islamic Texts Society, 1992), 30–31, 32, 57–59. Reprinted with the kind permission of the Islamic Texts Society. For the Building Bridges Seminar's previous consideration of al-Ghazālī's *The Ninety-Nine Beautiful Names of God* (and "al-Malik" in particular), see Lucinda Mosher, ed., *Freedom: Christian and Muslim Perspectives* (Washington, DC: Georgetown University Press, 2021), 55–56, 62–64.

5. Translation (as used by the Building Bridges Seminar, 2021) by Yousef Casewit, reprinted with his permission. See also Yousef Casewit, trans., *In the Names of God: A Mystical Theology of the Divine Names in the Qurʾān by the North African Sufi ʿAfīf al-Dīn al-Tilimsānī (d. 690/1291)* (New York: New York University Press, Library of Arabic Literature, 2023).

Part Three

Naming God in Devotional Practice

9

Naming God in Christian Prayer and Worship

Its Impact on Spiritual Formation

Lucy Gardner

Orientations: My Own Formational Experiences of Naming God in Devotion

The Christian liturgies in which I was nurtured—Holy Communion, Morning Prayer, and Evensong from the Church of England's *Book of Common Prayer*, alongside the texts for the Eucharist in its *Alternative Service Book*—favored two Names for God above all: "Almighty God" and "Heavenly Father."[1] The first perhaps represents a general, natural identification of God; the God Who might be discovered in philosophical contemplation of the very fact of the universe. The second, by contrast, clearly reflects the particular Name—Abba—revealed by Christ in His speech with and about the One He called Father, commended to His disciples as the preferred form of prayer to this Father of His, regarded as the general pattern for Christian prayer, and preserved as a precious core Christian prayer in what became known as "the Lord's Prayer."[2] Often placed directly side by side—"Almighty God, our Heavenly Father"—each Name modulates or glosses the other, together explaining "this God is that God" while also neatly setting out something of the tensions between far and near, transcendent and immanent, emotionally distant and personally intimate, unknown—unknowable even—yet known, to be negotiated in any practice of calling upon God by Name.

These two dominant titles jostled for attention alongside "the Lord" and a myriad of other intriguing personal, relational, metaphorical, and performative Names from the Psalms, some other Old Testament texts, and New Testament Canticles following the form of Hebrew hymns.[3] These titles enable this pattern of naming to span another tension: on the one hand, the use of Hebrew thought-forms, poetic structures, and vocabulary clearly establishes unity and continuity with Israelite worship, identifying the God and Father of our Lord Jesus Christ as the Holy One of Israel, revealed in the Old Testament as in fact God of the Universe; on the other hand, dwelling within the language and mindset of the Psalms requires the worshipper to frame contemplation and invocation of the divine majesty within the disturbing invitatory intimacy of prayer in the first-person singular—*my* Rock, *my* Strong Tower, *my* Portion. It is surely comforting to learn that the divine Lord of the Universe, in Whose honor and glory I delight, is on my side (Ps. 118:6) and has put my tears into His bottle (Ps. 56:8); just as it is wonderful to know that the Lord has fulfilled His promises and redeemed His people, and that this Promise-keeper will be the Dayspring from on high to guide our feet into the way of peace (as in the *Benedictus* Luke 1:68–79); at the same time, it is potentially alarming to reflect that this same mighty Lord, with Whom I regularly plead for mercy, understands my thoughts from afar, knows my softest, my most inward parts, beholds my going down and my rising up (all from Ps. 139), and even counts every hair on my head (Matt. 10:30).

To these Names for God were also added a similarly rich series of titles in hymnody addressed to Christ, reflecting the conviction of Philippians 2:9, that the Name above every name has been bestowed upon Jesus, and echoing a range of New Testament theological themes and devotional language. This locates the act of naming Christ securely within the psalmic tradition of divine naming (both by general pattern and by transposition of particular titles); it also builds upon the generative and even playful character of that tradition in a way that extends the list of divine titles available to worshippers.[4]

On rare and particularly solemn occasions, the Holy Spirit would also be the direct object of adoration and invocation, as in the various translations of the Latin hymn *Veni creator spiritus*, such as John Cosin's *Come Holy Ghost Our Souls Inspire*, often used at ordinations.[5] These and others added a new series of Names to the divine titles to be deployed in Christian worship, including Paraclete, Advocate, and Comforter (translations of the *parakletos* of John's gospel), Anointing Spirit, Breath of God, Immortal Love, Joy, Peace, and Love Divine.[6]

Finally, there were also hymns and prayers addressed to the Trinity as a whole. I belonged at school to the House of the Holy, Blessed and Glorious Trinity; our school prayer (by Geoffrey Roberts) ran:

Grant, O Most Glorious Trinity,
that as this school has been founded to Thy glory,

so it may forever flourish to Thy perpetual praise,
Who livest and reignest, our Light and our Salvation,
God ever blest, world without end. Amen.

Common on celebrations of Trinity Sunday would be Walter C. Smith's *Immortal, Invisible, God Only Wise*, with its subtle threefold invocation also evoking the ineffability of God alongside the clear identification of that threefold God with "the Ancient of Days" (compare, for example, to Dan. 7:13) and Reginald Heber's *Holy, Holy, Holy, Lord God Almighty*.[7] At mission services on the beach, I met William Whiting's rousing *Eternal Father, Strong to Save* with a verse addressed to each Person of the Trinity, and at college I discovered Cecil F. Alexander's stimulating translation of the challengingly alien yet strangely familiar *S. Patrick's Breastplate*.[8] Almost all recitations of the Psalms, most prayers, and many hymns would end with some form of Trinitarian doxology, and intercessions increasingly came to be addressed explicitly "to the Father, through the Son and in the power of the Spirit," emphasizing that prayers and praises were all being addressed to the God Who is Trinity, that these three Names belong inseparably to each other, and that they in some sense are how Christians name God.[9]

My personal formational experiences of Christian worship are of course neither normative nor representative, but I hope that outlining some of them may allow helpful illumination of the assumptions and connections that will be made and explored in what follows.

Christian poets, theologians, liturgists, and hymn writers alike have explored many ways to name God, building on scriptural tradition, reaching for refreshing ways to encapsulate the often originally challenging and shocking heart of many traditional images, and so the list of available words and imaginative vocabulary for naming and addressing God has grown. The list is by its very nature too long to exhaust. This inexhaustibility itself indicates something of the infinite and ineffable character of the God Christians seek in prayer and worship; it also provides an important insight into the unceasing and demanding character of human attempts to name and address that God.[10] My purpose here is not to provide a guide to different types of Christian Names for God, nor to use liturgical naming as a resource for the doctrine of God. I simply hope to sketch some aspects of the *activity* of using the Divine Names and to reflect upon what Christians—and possibly others—are doing (or what we might think we are doing) and what (we think) is happening, when we deploy these many Names for God in devotion.

Psalm 105 speaks of "calling upon God's Name" (v. 1), of "remembering His wonderful words" (v. 2), of "making known His deeds" (v. 1) and "telling of His wonderful works" (v. 5), of "seeking the LORD" (v. 4), "seeking His presence" (v. 4), and "glorying in His holy Name" (v. 3). Here I wish to explore what such activities look like, and the work they do within the context of Christian prayer and worship.[11] In this Janet Martin Soskice (among others) has been an invaluable guide in her reminders that the Names of God do not stand merely as condensed, coded statements about God and God's attributes but also work to establish and nurture our relationship to the Divine.[12] I hope to provide a taste of how the naming of God happens in Christian prayer and worship, and to reflect a little on ways in which that contributes to Christian spiritual formation.

The Many Names of God: Identifying, Confessing, Recalling, Reciting, Listing

The activity of naming anything, anyone, is an act of identifying it, or them, in contrast to other objects, other people, possessing different names. Naming God in prayer and worship serves to identify God. Nurturing a reverent respect for the disclosure afforded to Moses in the encounter at the burning bush (Exodus 3), Christian theology has developed a strong sense that the Divine Name YHWH ("I am Who I am" or "I am Who I will be") is a Name like no other. It refuses to sit still and behave like other names, and thus asserts the sheer mysterious, gratuitous being and continuing to be of the Being One Who thus names Itself. This teaches the important sense in which we cannot in fact name God, coupled with the sense that the gift of this Name, and thus our use of it, insists on a fundamental commitment to the fact that we can only name God because God has shared the Divine Name with us; fundamentally, in Christian devotion—as in Christian theology, the history of religion, and the history of salvation—it is God Who names God.

In the Christian, as in the Hebraic, understanding, God nevertheless also has given us other Names, other identifiers, that work in a manner more akin to other names: He is the God of Abraham, the God of Isaac, and the God of Jacob; God is our Strength and our Shield; God is the Holy One of Israel; God is the Most High; God is our Father, and God is also the maternal Rock Who bore us; God is my Tower and my Shield; God is Wisdom, Love and Justice; God is the Son, and God is the Spirit; and God the Son is the Door, and the Way, the Lamb and the Shepherd, the Bread of Life, the Living Water and the Vine, the Priest and the Victim. These God-given Names for God, and many more like them from scripture, are more than images that present a little knowledge of the otherwise unknown and unknowable God. They identify and in some sense locate God's identity for us, differentiating Him from Ba'al and Astaroth and any other putative gods.

They also serve to identify the worshipper, placing her in relation to God and in relation to other worshippers. If this God of Abraham and Isaac and Jacob is my God, then I have become part of their family. If God is my Father and the Rock Who bore me, then I am God's child; God's Son and all other children of God have become my brothers and sisters. If God is my Tower and my Shield, then God is my defense against all assaults of my enemies. If God is a Shepherd, then I am one of the precious, wayward sheep; if God is the Door, then I am looking for a way into the fold; if God is the Way, then I am a traveler; if God is the Truth, then I am a seeker after truth; if God is the Bread of Life, then the worshippers are those who hunger; if God is Living Water, then those who worship thirst; if God is the Vine, then His followers are the branches (and neither the grapes nor the wine-drinkers); if God is the Priest and the Victim, then the congregations becomes the benefactors of the sacrifice. Naming God in this way tells me who I am, tells Christians who we as worshippers are—offspring of Abraham, servants of God, children of Jacob, the chosen, cherished children of God, brothers and sisters of Jesus Christ, members of His Body.

This is the logic of confession: I acknowledge Who God is and, thus, Who I and my fellow worshippers learn ourselves to be. Naming God the God of Abraham, of Isaac and Jacob, of Sarah, Rebecca, and Rachel confesses and acknowledges God's election of and involvement in the life of Israel. Naming Jesus as "LORD" brings Him into this history, acknowledging not only that He has a key part to play but that He is in fact in some way to be identified with God, for this title unavoidably echoes the Septuagint's circumlocution for the Divine Name. To address Christ thus in worship does not merely repeat or simply obey the scriptural proclamation that "at the Name of Jesus, every knee should bow" (as in Phil. 2:10); it is part of accepting this revealed identity, making myself subject to it, owning it, confessing and proclaiming it as a fact that is determinative of who I understand myself to be and of Who I understand God to be.

Christian devotion follows another Hebrew Bible pattern in frequently recalling God's past deeds. This includes using events from God's dealings with Israel to tell the life of Christ, the life of the Church, or, indeed, the situation and hopes of the believer. Collects and other prayers often begin with a short direct address to God by Name, followed by a clause detailing something that God has done or regularly does, and that is relevant for the day or the prayer being offered.[13] Here, Naming God participates in recalling the wondrous deeds God has done, not only because such a telling requires the use of a name but also because the biblical Names for God themselves capture these deeds: God is hailed as Shield and Rock, as Defender and Redeemer, because He has revealed these as His Names in His dealings with Israel by establishing, shielding, defending, and redeeming them. Who God is and What God does are intimately connected, and the many Names of God serve to teach this point.[14] They also serve to teach the believing community—and any others prepared to listen—the story of God's dealings with the world, with Israel, with the peoples, and with the Church. This in turn again provides worshippers with a narrative sense of their own identity, as they are shown to have a place within that story, and therefore reassured (and warned!) that there is a place for them (their hopes and their fears, their successes and all the disasters they might meet) in God's good plans.

Rehearsing revelation in this way also serves to reclaim the realities of a sure and firm foundation for faith in this God, and for trust that we are loved. For, importantly, this rehearsal and the Names that belong with it reveal God primarily as Oath-keeper and Covenant-holder, always true not only to His Word but to Himself; Christian faith is grounded in God's own faithfulness. This teaches a trusting attitude to God that reaches not only into the past but is relevant for the present—for example, God is addressed as "Creator of the stars of night, Thy people's everlasting light" at the opening for an evening hymn, and as "Eternal Glory of the Sky, Blest hope of frail humanity" at the beginning of a hymn for the morning. It also provides the possibility and structure of hope for the future; Christian hope is likewise grounded in God's constancy and faithfulness.

Names can also be listed, and the many Names of God are often recited in prayer and worship. Compared to everyday use of names in other speech, this can seem initially an odd, arcane practice, perhaps worryingly akin to magic, but at least two potentially instructive and contrasting analogs can nevertheless be found. First there is the listing of royal names and legal titles afforded to noble persons in royal proclamations, deeds, and other legal documents.[15] These serve to set out who the person is in relation to many others, across a series of geographical locations and a range of social spheres. Such proclamations are also frequently peppered with flattering sentiments clearly intended to endorse the noble character of these personages, asserting their worthiness of these titles. Importantly, then, these lists can serve both to name, proclaim, and even claim these realities, on the one hand, and also to acknowledge them, pay some kind of tribute to them, and even grant them, on the other.[16]

Listing God's many Names and titles in prayer and worship clearly follows a similar pattern, establishing the full extent of God's lordship in creation along with something of its pattern and His character. When such lists use and echo biblical listings and other biblical material—words found, that is, in the Word of God—they give fresh voice (even if only silently in the human heart) to God's proclamation of God's Names, titles, powers, and dominion as King of all Kings, LORD of all Lords, and they set out His superlatively royal, noble, trustworthy, powerful character on the way. In reciting these lists, worshippers confess and acknowledge all this, resonating with the second petition of the Lord's Prayer, "Thy will be done, in earth as it is in Heaven." The application of such a listing to the Second Person of the Trinity, its transferral to Christ, can be read, for example, as the frame for Matthew Bridges's hymn, *Crown Him with Many Crowns*, in which Christ is named by a series of titles drawn from Israel's history and the New Testament's reflections on His life.

But it is perhaps more often in the tender intimacy of the soothing words that pass between lover and beloved, devoted friend and companion, or loving parent and infant child that we encounter lists of name upon name in our nonliturgical speech, uttered not in attempts to express the dizzying heights of impressive power but rather in the ceaseless endeavor to give expression to the inexhaustible, inexpressible length and breadth and depth of love.[17] Our recitations of Divine Names do not merely seek to proclaim and acknowledge God's power in humble obeisance; they also play an important part in the simple act of loving devotion as part of our attempts to learn to love God. Something of this loving delight with which the Name of God may inspire the worshipper is captured in John Newton's hymn, *How Sweet the Name of Jesus Sounds*, which includes a stanza composed almost entirely of a list of Names for Jesus:

> O Jesus, Shepherd, Guardian, Friend,
> my Prophet, Priest, and King,
> My Lord, my Life, my Way, my End,
> accept the praise I bring.

The sheer number and variety of the Names of God deployed in this way resonate with the disorienting rhetoric of the Name revealed at the burning bush, collectively insisting on each one's inability to point and say, "Look, this thing is God," or "See now, God is this thing": if God is both Father *and* the Rock who bears us, both Lamb and Shepherd, both Bread and Water, then of course God is quite simply not *literally* any of these things. By the same token, since these Names also locate and identify worshippers, in listing them we discover we are not limited to mono-dimensional relationships with God: we can move, often abruptly, between offspring, bride, and sibling; between vine branches, sheep, and warriors; between comforted and challenged as in devotion we explore who we are and God's meaning for our lives.

These lists are notoriously unstable, never-ending, always generating new Names. Even those lists that propose a certain, often holy, number seem constantly in search of their correct members, containing different items in their various iterations.[18] This, too, echoes within the ultimately ungraspable nature of the Divine Name and its gesture toward the essential fact that we cannot simply name God and, indeed, simply cannot do so at all apart from God's decision to grant us the precious gifts of Names with which to address Him. This in turn casts an informative light on the nature of the many types of repetition encountered in both liturgical and extemporary prayer, for it enables them to be seen as a reflection in finitude of the infinite qualities of the One we seek to address.

The Power of God's Name: Evoking, Addressing, Invoking, Protecting

Names can also evoke, bringing to mind various associations, patterns of experience, and networks of thought. Similarly, the Names of God can tell us something of what God is *like*: if God is the Holy One, then God is holy; if God is Wisdom, then God is wise; if God is Justice, then God is just. Named as Father or Mother, God is seen as generative, tender, loving, concerned for our good, perhaps stern, and in some sense set over us. Named as Spouse or Sibling, God is perceived as loving in a different way, jealous possibly, desiring us ourselves, and in some sense a companion set alongside us. In calling out God's Names in devotion, then, we evoke different networks of experience and meaning with which to associate God, exploring Who God is and What God is like, along with our growing understandings of what that means for our lives and who we are. We summon these aspects and images of God as the backdrop and horizon for our lives.

God's gracious gift of His Names—in Word and deed—enables us to address the otherwise unknown God. Names are useful for talking about something or someone in the third person, and this is often how the Names of God are regarded and analyzed in philosophy and theology. In prayer and worship, however, the use of the third person for God is usually contained within second-person address: even when we are taking *about* God in devotional speech, we are usually already talking *to* God. Here the Names of God have the power to call God into a dialogue, engaging Him in conversation, prompting Him to action even, and different Names will be deployed for different modes of engagement. But, critically here, these human acts of addressing God are always only ever response to the God Who, historically as well as theologically, has always spoken first, not only in the prophets and the history of Israel but in the very act of speaking creation into existence, and of course for Christians in the Life and Person of Jesus Christ. Christian devotion is structured in dialogue form; the Names we use are often repetitions and recastings of the Names that God has given us, and, indeed, the very words and prayers we speak are words contained in scriptural revelation: Christian worship answers God with God's own words.

Christian devotion also invokes God, calling upon Him, calling upon the power of His Name. Both worship and preaching often begin with the phrase "In the Name of the Father, and of the Son, and of the Holy Spirit"; prayers are offered "in Christ's Name"; absolution is pronounced by those ordained to do so in God's Name; exorcisms depend upon the Divine Name; reproofs, prophecies, and blessings are offered in God's Name; and the congregation is sent out at the end of worship in God's Name. Here we see practical instances of belief in the power of God's Name offered not only as a convenient circumlocution for the power of God but embedded in rhetoric and experience of the mysterious way in which God's gift of His Names is in fact part of His gift of Himself. Cautiously following Sergei Bulgakov's creative suggestions here, we might think of the Names of God as "verbal icons of God."[19] More than keys, or doors, or windows onto What and Who God is, the Names for God that God has so generously shared with and bestowed upon His people are God's act of identifying Himself and so in some extended sense part of sharing His identity; these Names of God are therefore bearers of God's power.[20]

The Names chosen to address and invoke God in will often be linked to the context of worship, or what the worshipper is asking of God. Drawing parallels between the worshipper journeying through the struggles of life and Israel's years in the wilderness, William Williams prays, for example, for guidance, manna, water, deliverance, comfort, and safety from Jehovah, the Redeemer, Bread of Heaven, Strong Deliverer, who is Death of Death and Hell's Destruction in his much loved *Guide Me, O Thou Great Jehovah / Redeemer.*[21] In the Advent antiphons, the congregation calls on Christ-Wisdom to teach them, on Christ the Lord and Leader of Israel to redeem them, on Christ the Radiant Dawn and Sun of Righteousness to bring them enlightenment, and so on.[22] Collects and other prayers often begin with a short direct address to God by Name, followed by a clause detailing something that God has done or regularly does as a prelude to asking God to perform a similar action in the present or the future.[23] Where recalling and remembering provide the basis for faith and hope, invocation gives a fuller, practical expression to that hope, embodying the expectation that the Oath-keeper will be true to His promises and His covenant, confident that He will indeed keep His Word.[24]

In considering Christian invocation of God, then, we see faith at work and glimpse something of the theme of Christian audacity.[25] When we place reverent faith in God's Name, explains St. Augustine, we shall discover its power: when spoken "with respect for the greatness of [God's] majesty," it is found to be great, and when spoken "with veneration and fear of offending Him," it is found to be holy.[26] We can, that is, call upon God's Name and invoke its real power to profound effects and to good; by implication, we can also speak it with disdain and irreverence when we might find its real power for devastation. Although the invocation of God's Name as a faithful calling upon God's power and a trusting reliance upon God to act is a persistent feature of Christian worship, extensions of this use are contentious, recognized as dangerous, potentially falling foul of the second and third commandments (against idolatry, and against taking the LORD's Name in vain, Exod. 20:4–7; Deut. 8:5–11) and succumbing to the temptations of magicalism and superstition.[27] Yet the very fact that such uses need to be warned against and forbidden demonstrates their real possibility and potential attraction. The demarcation between using God's Name and its power as part of placing our trust in God, on the one hand, and seeking to overreach that gift and ourselves by taking it as a power to wield ourselves to our own ends, on the other, needs therefore to be fiercely guarded.

The use of Christ's Name in Christian prayer builds not only on Philippians 2 but on the declaration to the disciples that when two or three gather in His Name, Christ is with them (Matt. 18:10) and the promises that whatever they ask in His Name will be given them (cf., e.g., Mark 11:24; Matt. 21:22; John 14:13). These clearly both convey a sense of the power of Christ's Name to make Him present and to win success for worshippers' petitions. Christ also promises His disciples that using His Name they will be able to cast out demons, speak in tongues, pick up snakes, withstand poison, and heal the sick (Mark 16:17–18).[28]

Whatever the precise interpretations of how these promises translate into contemporary practice, every community must struggle with the times when Christ's Name has been uttered but His presence has not been felt, His disciples have not felt its protection or been able to heal the sick, and with prayer requests that have pronounced in His Name but do not appear to have been given whatever they asked. One solution is to suggest that the Name was not spoken properly, or with enough faith, but this risks locating power not in the Name itself but in the human practices surrounding it, thus relocating faith not in the Name, not in God, and not in God's power but in human capacity, skill, and virtuosity. Another, more demanding, more cautious, but perhaps more satisfactory, approach is to attend to the wider context of these scriptural promises. In John's writings, for example, they are clearly anchored in the delivery of Christ's "new commandment" to His disciples to love one another with the love that He has shown them; they are also connected with His exposition of how the mutual indwelling He enjoys with the Father and the Holy Spirit is extended to include His followers.

Here we begin to see that "gathering in the Name of Christ" and "asking in Christ's Name" are not just about voicing particularly powerful words or uttering magical sounds but about seeking to align what we want with what God wants, seeking God's will above our own. Liturgically, spiritually, then, meeting "in Christ's Name" becomes thankfully remembering Christ's love (and especially His loving sacrifice of Himself at the Last Supper and on the cross, centrally in the celebration of the Eucharist, the congregation's participation in Christ's prayer of thanks to the Father). "Asking in Christ's Name" becomes praying Christ's prayer to His Father in Heaven: the "not my will but thine be done" (Luke 22:42) in Gethsemane before the completion of that sacrifice, and the "Thy Kingdom come, Thy will be done" in the pattern of prayer commended to the disciples and adopted as the constant prayer of the Church. And seeking to perform wonders in Christ's Name becomes a particular request, a particular faith in Christ, to extend His life-saving protection and healing to those prayed for, even when these benefits take spiritual rather than physical form.

The power of God's Name can also be seen in the theme of protection. Psalm 20:1 prays may "the Name of the God of Jacob protect you!" and Proverbs 18:10 teaches that "the Name of the Lord is a strong tower." Throughout scripture and in Christian worship, God is presented in Names and vocabulary related to shielding and protecting—Refuge and Tower, Shield and Defender. This is a quality, an attribute, on which the worshipper may call in seeking God's protection. More than that, in these and other verses, this quality is extended (some might say "transferred") to God's Name(s). More than a powerful tool to deploy, then, God's Name itself offers shelter: as shade from the sun, a roof against the rain, a shield against the wind, a tender, loving wing against predators, God's Name is a safe place, somewhere we can hide. In Christian worship, especially Eucharistic devotion, Christ Himself, and particularly His body and His wounds, become this safe, sheltering, mothering space.[29] The power of God's Name as Trinity to protect is likewise invoked in hymns and prayers such as *St. Patrick's Breastplate.*

The Glory of God's Name: Dwelling, Exploring, Straining, Seeking, Honoring

> Blessed be the Name of the LORD
> from this time forth and for evermore. (Ps. 113:2)

Whether uttered in the silent solitude of the heart, mumbled in a small gathering for early morning service, spoken in the extended congregation of a live-streamed service, sung out in awe-inspiring choral settings in cathedral evensong, or chanted with a busy, noisy cast of hundreds at a megachurch, the use of God's Names in Christian devotion is always participation in the community of the Church through the ages and across the nations, joining in the praise of the Communion of Saints, uniting Heaven and earth.[30]

More than this, however, Christian prayer and worship are also always in some sense a participation in God. Building on the theme of shelter, we can see the gift of God's many Names as creating a framework, a house in which we can dwell and within which we can also set about seeking the LORD and exploring the infinite mystery of God. Here we learn of the Names of God as things to delight in; we can cautiously begin to interpret what Psalm 105:3 might mean in its exhortation to "Glory in [God's] holy Name." The lists we recite, the prayers we pray, the hymns we sing, begin to "play" with the Names and ideas that God has given us, straining language to express what it can never capture, striving to understand God's Names better, creatively devising new ways to rediscover and re-present their once novel and disorienting impact, exploring the ways in which they always point beyond human language, knowledge, and understanding, as we seek to know God better, and hunt ever new ways into His presence. This straining playfulness takes different forms in different cultures but is recognizable in the riddle-like kennings of Old English and Old Norse poetry, for example, as in the strange-familiar turns of phrase in works by John Donne, Anna Laetitia Barbauld, Gerard Manley Hopkins, and T. S. Eliot.[31] It can be discovered in the creative, imaginative attributions collated in John Mbiti's list of African Names for Jesus, as in the prayers of St. Ephrem and the mystics.[32] It appears in the long list of simple appellations for Christ in the *Litany of the Most Holy Name of Jesus* and is found in the simplicity of many favorite worship songs in contemporary Evangelicalism.[33] The idea that it is the *many* Names of God—and their often crudely metaphorical nature and sometimes abrasive juxtapositions—that enable us to name the unnamable God at all is no merely ancient wisdom but a lively and current practice.[34]

The power of the Names of God to make people part of this community, however, extends beyond establishing an intellectual, moral, or even spiritual connection with others who use and have used the same Names. Being baptized "in the Name of the Father, and of the Son, and of the Holy Spirit" makes a person sacramentally (we might say ontologically) part of the Church, part of Christ, a member of His Body. Here we see something of another aspect in which the Naming of God in Christian prayer and worship brings with it a further important dimension of participation. Since it is only God Who names God, when worshippers use those God-given Names, and the many human translations and creations inspired by them, we participate in a Divine activity, and thus in God. Christian worship does not only understand itself as responding to the God Who has first addressed us; it is conceived and experienced as participation in the divine eternal conversation within the Godhead itself. If I call God YHWH, or Blessed Lord, or Mighty Warrior, or any other Name from the tradition, then I speak God's Name but I also speak God's words, mine animated by Him.[35] If I call Christ "Son of God," then my words resonate within the Father's eternal naming of the Logos as "First Begotten," and within His declaration at Christ's baptism, "This is my Son, my Beloved" (Matt. 3:17). If I call God "Father," then I join in Christ's, the Son's, loving address of His beloved "Abba," and indeed I am only enabled to do so in, through, and by the power of the Holy Spirit working, and groaning, and sighing within me to do so (Rom. 8).[36]

Finally, we come to what perhaps should in a sense always be the first word on the place of the Name of God in Christian prayer and worship: the positive implied in the negative of the third commandment, and an exploration of the meaning of the first petition of the Lord's Prayer: "hallowed be thy Name." The Names of the Lord might teach us, form us, protect us, and challenge us, but ultimately, initially, they are given for us to revere and respect, and in revering and respecting them, to bless and hallow, adore and praise, worship and give thanks to God—Who needs none of these things, to Whom none of these things can be added, and yet Who longs for us to make this move, and direct our gaze and our hearts, our minds and our lives to Him in love (an unselfish love that will paradoxically prove to be for our own benefit!). Here, alongside the lessons in faith and hope, we see learning and worshipping God's Name as a structure for a training in love, the love of God that spills over into a love of other objects of God's love, a love of neighbor, a love of stranger, a love of creation, and even a love of enemy.[37]

All Christian traditions take the injunction to honor God's Holy Name seriously, but it is expressed physically in worship in many different ways: for example, bowing the head or removing a liturgical head-covering at the mention of the Name of "Jesus"; crossing oneself at invocation of the Trinity or bowing for a Trinitarian doxology; raising hands in the air when addressing God by Name or invoking His majesty; and kneeling or prostrating to pray in humility before God. These actions are not promoted as meritorious in their own right but commended as ways in which physical creatures can pay due reverence to God through reverence for God's Name and as ways in which the body can anchor the mind and heart in prayer, teaching the soul and, indeed, the whole human person his or her true origin, proper orientation, and final end: God's Name and, indeed, God Himself, as the map, the terrain, and the compass upon which our whole lives depend.

Conclusion: God's Name in Christian Spiritual Formation

These different aspects of naming God in Christian devotion thus locate worshippers in a narrative that makes sense of the present by weaving complex connections between their past and their future. They also provide a training in the theological virtues of faith, hope, and love. The trajectory, the goal, of the Christian spiritual life is to be transformed by the Holy Spirit, reformed in the image of God, by being conformed to Christ (Rom. 8).[38] In learning and using God's Names in prayer and worship, we discover God as Almighty Creator, and ourselves as tiny creatures; we meet God as Holy Justice, and find ourselves to be miserable sinners; we meet God as Father and Spouse and delight in finding that we are precious loved ones. Likewise, in encountering Christ as "my Lord and my God" (John 20:28), I find myself not only a child of God but a sister of God, and in discovering that Jesus is not only Teacher but Friend, I discover myself accompanied by God.

But the gift of God's Names does not merely teach us Who God is and who we are in turn. God's Name does not only reveal and judge; it has the power to effect changes in our circumstances: to bring healing, to give blessings, to make our prayer acceptable, to draw us closer to Him. And it has the power to transform us, softening our hearts of stone, converting our minds and wills, re-creating us according to His good will, restoring His image in us. We are given God's Names to use reverently; this is part of God's good will for us, that we should worship Him, not because this is what He deserves (although He does), not because this adds anything to God (how could it?), but because this is His good pleasure: that we should enjoy His presence and share His life, His peace, and His joy with Him forever. Devotion is good for us, not for God; it teaches us the theological virtues of faith, hope, and love. And it is our ultimate, destiny, our goal, the good portion allotted to us. In the Christian revelation, devotion is uncovered as the route to reaching that goal. Hallowing God's Name, Glorying in God's Name, is the path that leads us to the future through our connection to the past and ultimately to the joyful future intended for us in which we shall share in praising God eternally.

For Christians, this is inextricably connected with God's Name as Trinity, Father, Son, and Holy Spirit, and conceived in irreducibly Trinitarian terms: the intended future for God's people is taking their appropriate place participating in God as Love, eternally adoring the Father, in the power of the Spirit, and in union with Christ. By attempting to orient ourselves to and by God's Holy Name, we cooperate with the Holy Spirit's re-creation of us in God's image and His incorporation of us into the Divine Life by His drawing us into the Son's eternal thanksgiving prayer to the Father, and into the union between God and humanity, which has already occurred in the incarnation of that eternal Word. It is not, however, necessarily unthinkable that aspects of this pattern and the realities it reflects can be known under other Names of God or experienced in other devotional practices, which provides a starting point at least for Christians to engage with understanding how God is named and worshipped in other faith traditions, and especially one that also calls on the God of Abraham and Sarah, as on the God of Jesus.

Notes

1. The tendency of mainstream English Anglicanism to rely so heavily on just these two particular titles has (thankfully) receded significantly with the arrival of a greater breadth of available and authorized liturgical material, offered both "from the ground up" (such as in the work of Janet Morley) and "from the center" in the development and collation of the rich resources of *Common Worship*. See, for example, Janet Morley, *All Desires Known*, 3rd ed. (New York: Church Publishing, 2006); and Janet Morley, ed., *Bread of Tomorrow: Prayers for the Church Year* (Maryknoll, NY: Orbis, 1992).

2. On Christ's speech *with* His Father, compare, for example, John 17; Luke 23:34 and 46; Matthew 26:39. On Christ's speech *about* His Father, compare, for example, John 5:19; John 14; Matthew 7:21. The Lord's Prayer is delivered in two slightly different forms at Matthew 6:5–15 and Luke 11:1–13. The traditional liturgical form is closest to Matthew's:

> Our Father, Who art in Heaven, hallowed be Thy Name;
> Thy Kingdom come, Thy will be done, in earth as it is in Heaven.
> Give us this day our daily bread.
> And forgive us our trespasses, as we forgive them that trespass against us.
> And lead us not into temptation, but deliver us from evil.

3. On personal Names, for example, "my King" (Ps. 5:2), "a Judge" (Ps. 7:11). On relational Names, for example, "the God of Jacob" (Ps. 20:1), "the God of Abraham" (Ps. 47:9). On metaphorical Names, for example, "my Rock" (Ps. 31:3), "my Shield" (Ps. 3:3), "my Stronghold" (Ps. 144:2). On performative Names, for example, "my Deliverer" (Ps. 40:17; 144:2).

4. Examples include the Advent Antiphons and Naida Hearn's *Jesus, Name above All Names* (which, as sung by Terry Macalmon, can be found here: https://www.youtube.com/watch?v=oZY4mizHzoo), but also Matthew Bridges's *Crown Him with Many Crowns* and George H. Bourne's *Lord Enthroned in Heav'nly Splendor*, the full text of which is available at Hymnary.org.

5. The full texts of Cosin's *Come Holy Ghost Our Souls Inspire* is available at Hymnary.org; other translations include Edward Caswall's *Come, Holy Ghost, Creator Blest*, Robert II of France's *Come Holy Ghost in Love*, and Charles Wesley's *Come, Holy Ghost, Our Hearts Inspire*. Again, see Hymnary.org.

6. Examples include Isaac Watt's *Come, Holy Spirit, Heavenly Dove* and Samuel Longfellow's *Holy Spirit, Truth Divine*. See Hymnary.org.

7. The full texts of Smith's *Immortal, Invisible, God Only Wise* and Heber's *Holy, Holy, Holy, Lord God Almighty* are available at Hymnal.net.

8. The full text of Whiting's *Eternal Father, Strong to Save* is available at Hymnary.org. For Alexander's *S. Patrick's Breastplate*, see the texts for study provided in the next chapter of this volume.

9. Most commonly, the Trinitarian doxology is "Glory be to the Father, and to the Son, and to the Holy Ghost, as it was in the beginning, is now and ever shall be, world without end. Amen," for Psalms and Canticles, and "through Jesus Christ, Thy Son our Lord, who liveth and reigneth with Thee, in the unity of the Holy Ghost, ever one God, world without end. Amen," for collects and other prayers. "To the Father, through the Son and in the power of the Spirit" echoes the description of the pattern of Christian prayer found, for example, in Romans 8:15–17: "When we cry, 'Abba!, Father,' it is the . . . Spirit bearing witness with our spirit that we are children of God . . . and coheirs with Christ."

10. As encapsulated in St. Augustine's famous dictum *si enim comprehendis, non est Deus* ("If you understand, it is not God"). See his *Sermons* 117:5.

11. My list will not be exhaustive; it deliberately eschews any semblance of providing a survey of all the very many different practices surrounding the use of God's Names in Christian prayer and worship. Nor, in seeking to explore some aspects of the activity of Naming God in prayer and worship, do I wish to propose that each is entirely separate and discrete from the others, just as when Christians proclaim *Laudámus te, benedícimus te, adorámus te, glorificámus te* (rendered rather weakly as "we worship you, we give you thanks, we praise you for your glory," in English) in the *Gloria*, they are using different viewpoints to describe the one activity in which they are engaging, rather than merely listing a series of separate jobs to be performed.

12. See, for example, Janet Martin Soskice, "Naming God: Or Why Names Are Not Attributes," in *New Blackfriars* 101, no. 1092 (March 2020):182–95; her inspiring exposition of the importance of *kinship* in Christian traditions of naming God throughout *The Kindness*

of God: Metaphor, Gender and Religious Language (Oxford: Oxford University Press, 2007), and her discussion of Divine Love in "Being and Love: Schleiermacher, Aquinas and Augustine" in *Modern Theology* 34, no. 3 (2018): 480–91.

13. For example, "Lord of all life and power, who through the mighty resurrection of your Son overcame the old order of sin and death" on Easter Day, "Gracious Father, who gave the first martyr Stephen grace to pray for those who took up stones against him" on St. Stephen's Day, or "Almighty God, you show to those who are in error the light of your truth, that they may return to the way of righteousness" on the Second Sunday of Lent in the Church of England's *Common Worship*.

14. Here I note that Christians have grown used to the insistence that we need to remember to connect the Person and Work of Christ in this manner but have fallen into epistemological tangles in trying to negotiate the same insight when considering the links between seeing God-at-work as Trinity in the economy of God's dealings with the world and contemplating the mystery of identifying God-as-God as Trinity.

15. One poignant reminder of this archaic practice in recent British culture was the recitation of his titles at the closing of the late Duke of Edinburgh's funeral.

16. A politically attentive reading of history will of course always want to question the precise balance between the proclamation and assertion on the one hand, and acknowledgement and acceptance on the other, particularly in situations where the latter is demanded by the former against the backdrop of threat, menace, and violent enforcement.

17. This parallel gains a particular valence when Christ is identified with the Bridegroom of the Song of Songs and other nuptial passages (in keeping with Ephesians 5) and the Church or, indeed, the individual worshipper is seen as His Bride; limitations of space sadly preclude attention to this theme in its own right here.

18. For an intriguing argument of this point, see Valentina Izmirlieva, *All the Names of the Lord: Lists, Mysticism, and Magic* (Chicago: University of Chicago Press, 2008).

19. Sergei Bulgakov, *Icons and the Name of God* (Grand Rapids, MI: Eerdmans, 2012), 135–36.

20. Bulgakov, 137.

21. One translation is available at Hymnary.org.

22. See texts for study provided in chapter 10 of this volume.

23. See note 13, above.

24. See also William Whiting's *Eternal Father Strong to Save*, which invokes each Person of the Trinity in turn, setting out particular instances in which each has demonstrated their shared power over the sea and united will to save as the basis and structure for the delivery of the repeated plea, "O hear us when we cry to thee, / for those in peril on the sea."

25. Compare 1 Corinthians 1:31; Jeremiah 9:24.

26. St. Augustine, *De serm. Dom. in monte* 2, 5, 19; *Patrologia Latina* 34, 1278; quoted at §2149 in *Catechism of the Catholic Church* (London: Geoffrey Chapman, 1994), 466.

27. Our focus here is restricted to prayer and worship, and while this in some sense includes ritual, we must forbear to explore lively concerns over the use and abuse of God's Name in inscription, which might be faithfully associated with delivering a blessing, or contrariwise treated as an amulet or talisman.

28. These three sets of promise also resonate with the meanings of two of Christ's Names, both of which link Him directly with God: "Jesus" itself (cognate with "Joshua") is linked to meanings such as "my salvation" (or even "God saves"; and even if the Divine is not etymologically captured in this Name, for the Hebrew Bible, it is *only* God Who can save); and "Immanuel" means God-with-us.

29. In J. Hegarty's *Soul of my Savior*, for example, the worshipper prays "Strength and protection may thy passion be . . . deep in thy wounds, Lord, hide and shelter me."

30. This sense of joining in the heavenly, angelic worship glimpsed in Isaiah and the book of Revelation is seen, for instance, in the introduction to the solemn praying of the *Sanctus* in the Eucharistic prayer with words such as, "Therefore with angels and archangels, and with all the company of heaven, we proclaim your great and glorious name, for ever praising you and saying: Holy, Holy, Holy Lord, God of power and might." *Common Worship* Eucharistic Prayer B.

31. For example, Mary's lament in the anonymous *Drápa af Máríugrát* describes God as "the mighty prince of the people of the moon's path" (people of the moon's path = angels), "the Lord of lightning's shrine," "Lord of the star hall." Text and translation available at Skaldic Poetry of the Scandinavian Middle Ages: https://skaldic.org/m.php?p=skaldic.

32. This list of 631 names of God in 102 African languages, as found in thirty African countries, is included in John S. Mbiti, *Concepts of God in Africa* (London: SPCK, 1970). For many years this list was also made available by the Maryknoll Language Institute (Musoko, Tanzania) as *African Names, Titles, Images, Descriptions, and Attributes of God.* It is now promulgated on several websites. See also John Mbiti, "List of Christological Titles of Jesus Christ in African Christianity," in *Missio Africanus Journal of African Missiology* 1, no. 2 (January 2016): 89–91. For a helpful treatment of Ephrem's use of paradox and symbolism in poetry to explore the boundless God within the constraints of language, see Sebastian P. Brock *The Luminous Eye: The Spiritual World Vision of St. Ephrem* (Rome: CIIS, 1985), 24–26.

33. Representative text available, for example, at the United States Conference of Catholic Bishops website, "Litany of the Holy Name of Jesus": https://www.usccb.org/prayers/litany-holy-name-jesus.

34. This point (which draws on Aquinas, in his turn drawing on Pseudo-Dionysius) is explored with insight by Rowan Williams in his discussion of language for God as a form of excessive speech in an extreme situation in poetry in his *The Edge of Words: God and the Habits of Language* (London: Continuum, 2014), 148–49. For reflections on how Aquinas also provides a basis for arguing that it is *how we use* the many Names for God as much as what they might individually say that contributes to their capacity to describe the indescribable God, see David Burrell, "Naming the Names of God: Muslims, Jews, Christians," *Theology Today* 47, no. 1 (1990): 2–29.

35. Services of Morning and Evening Prayer, for example, open with short dialogical prayers that begin with the call and response: "*Minister*: O Lord, open thou our lips. *People*: And our mouth shall shew forth thy praise."

36. Reflecting on the relationships between naming and recognizing God as Trinity, on the one hand, and understanding that and how God can be with His creatures, on the other,

Hans Urs von Balthasar suggests that it is precisely the fact that there is a "with-God" *in* God (between the Three Persons of the One God Christians nevertheless insist on addressing in the singular "Thou") that enables "God-with-us," a reference to one of the Names of Jesus ("Emmanuel"—Isa. 7:14; Matt. 1:23—means "God with us"), to happen within creation. See Hans Urs von Balthasar, *You Crown the Year with Your Goodness: Sermons through the Liturgical Year*, trans. Graham Harrison (San Francisco: Ignatius, 1989), 141–45.

37. Christ teaches the dual commandment of loving God and loving thy neighbor as oneself as the summary of the Torah (for example, Mark 12:29–31; see also Lev. 19:18), itself the first episode in God's revelation and dealings with Israel. That Torah, Israel's law, includes the injunction to love strangers (for example, Deut. 10:19), John's Gospel proclaims that God loves the world (John 3:16) and Christ teaches the extension of the love of neighbor to the love of one's enemies (Matt. 5:43–44). This firm linkage between loving God and loving neighbor is also explored as anchored in God as Love in 1 John 4; a passage in which the Trinitarian vocabulary of Father, Son, and Spirit is inextricably intertwined.

38. This Trinitarian pattern of Christian formation is also echoed in 1 John 4's intense exposition of God as Love and the way that is linked to the commandment to love, which also uses the Father, Son, Spirit language to describe how we are changed in loving.

10

Christian Devotional Literature on Naming God

Selections for Dialogue

Thomas Olivers (1725–99)

The God of Abraham Praise

A paraphrase of "Yigdal Elohim Hai," Daniel ben Judah's poem rehearsing the thirteen articles of Jewish belief outlined by Maimonides.

The God of Abraham praise
Who reigns enthroned above,
Ancient of everlasting days
And God of love:
To him uplift your voice,
At whose supreme command
From earth we rise, and seek the joys
At his right hand.

Though nature's strength decay,
And earth and hell withstand,
To Canaan's bounds we urge our way
At his command.
The watery deep we pass,
With Jesus in our view;
And through the howling wilderness
Our way pursue.

The goodly land we see,
With peace and plenty blest;
A land of sacred liberty

And endless rest;
There milk and honey flow
And oil and wine abound,
And trees of life forever grow,
With mercy crowned.

There dwells the Lord our King,
The Lord our Righteousness,
Triumphant o'er the world and sin,
The Prince of Peace;
On Sion's sacred height
His kingdom he maintains,
And glorious with his Saints in light
For ever reigns.

Before the great Three-One
They all exulting stand,
And tell the wonders he hath done
Through all their land:
The listening spheres attend,
And swell the growing fame,
And sing, in songs which never end,
The wondrous name.

The God who reigns on high
The great Archangels sing,
And "Holy, Holy. Holy," cry,
"Almighty King!
Who was, and is, the same,
And evermore shall be:
Eternal Father, great I am,
We worship thee."

Before the Savior's face
The ransomed nations bow,
O'erwhelmed at his almighty grace
For ever new;
He shows his prints of love,—
They kindle to a flame,

And sound through all the worlds above
The slaughtered Lamb.

The whole triumphant host
Give thanks to God on high;
"Hail! Father, Son, and Holy Ghost,"
They ever cry:
Hail Abraham's God, and mine!
(I join the heavenly lays)
All might and majesty are thine,
And endless praise. Amen.[1]

Latin (circa ninth century)

The Advent Antiphons

Also called the "O Antiphons," this series of calls to Christ by means of various ancient names to be recited before and after The Magnificat *(Mary's Song) at Vespers (Evening Prayer or Evensong). There is an antiphon for each of the last seven days before Christmas—the great feast of the Incarnation.*

O Sapientia, quae ex ore Altissimi prodisti, attingens a fine usque ad finem fortiter, suaviter disponensque omnia: veni ad docendum nos viam prudentiae.
O Adonai, et dux domus Israel, qui Moyse in igne flammae rubi apparuisti, et ei in Sina legem dedisti: veni ad redimendum nos in brachio extento.
O Radix Jesse, qui stas in signum populorum, super quem continebunt reges os suum, quem gentes deprecabuntur: veni ad liberandum nos, jam noli tardare.
O Clavis David, et sceptrum domus Israel, qui aperis, et nemo claudit; claudis, et nemo aperuit: veni, et educ vinctum de domo carceris, sedentem in tenebris, et umbra mortis.
O Oriens, splendor lucis aeternae, et sol justitiae: veni, et illumina sedentes in tenebris, et umbra mortis.
O Rex Gentium, et desideratus earum, lapisque angularis, qui facis utraque unum: veni, et salva hominem, quem de limo formasti.
O Emmanuel, Rex et Legifer noster, expectratio gentium, et Salvator earum: veni ad salvandum nos, Domines, Deus noster.

O Wisdom that comes out of the mouth of the Most High, and reaches from one end to another, mightily and sweetly ordering all things: Come and teach us the way of thy prudence.
O Adonai, and Leader of the house of Israel, who appeared in the Bush to Moses in a flame of fire, and gave him the Law in Sinai: Come and redeem us with an outstretched arm.
O Root of Jesse, that stands for an ensign of the people, before whom kings shall keep silence and to whom Gentiles shall make supplication: Come to deliver us; tarry not.
O Key of David, and Scepter of the House of Israel; who opens and no one shuts, who shuts and no one opens: Come and bring the prisoners out of the prison-house, they who sit in darkness and the shadow of death.
O Dayspring [Dawn], brightness of light everlasting, and sun of righteousness: Come and enlighten those who sit in darkness and the shadow of death.
O King of the Nations, and their desire; The Cornerstone who makes both one: Come and save humankind, whom You formed out of clay.
O Emmanuel [God with Us], our King and Lawgiver, the desire of all nations and their Salvation: Come and save us, O Lord our God.[2]

Attributed to St. Patrick (372–466)
Translation by Cecil Frances Alexander (1818–95)

St. Patrick's Breastplate

I bind unto myself today the strong name of the Trinity,
By invocation of the same, the Three in One, and One in Three.

I bind this day to me for ever, by power of faith, Christ's Incarnation;
His baptism in Jordan river: his death on cross for my salvation;
His bursting from the spiced tomb; His riding up the heavenly way;
His coming at the day of doom; I bind unto myself today.

I bind unto myself the power of the great love of Cherubim;
The sweet "Well done" in judgment hour; the service of the Seraphim,
Confessors' faith, Apostles' word, the Patriarchs' prayers, the Prophets' scrolls,
All good deeds done unto the Lord, and purity of virgin souls.

I bind unto myself today, the virtues of the star-lit heaven,
The glorious sun's life-giving ray, the whiteness of the moon at even,
The flashing of the lightning free, the whirling wind's tempestuous shocks,
The stable earth, the deep salt sea, around the old eternal rocks.

I bind unto myself today the power of God to hold and lead,
His eye to watch, his might to stay, His ear to hearken to my need.
The wisdom of my God to teach, His hand to guide, his shield to ward;
The word of God to give me speech, His heavenly host to be my guard.

Against the demon lures of sin, the vice that gives temptation force,
The natural lusts that lure within, the hostile men that mar my course;
Or few or many, or far or nigh, in every place, and in all hours,
Against their fierce hostility, I bind to me these holy powers.

Against all Satan's spells and wiles, against false words of heresy,
Against the knowledge that defiles, against the heart's idolatry,
Against the wizard's evil craft, against the death-wound and the burning,
The choking wave, the poisoned shaft, protect me Christ, till thy returning.

Christ be with me, Christ within me,
Christ behind me, Christ before me,
Christ beside me, Christ to win me,
Christ to comfort and restore me.
Christ beneath me, Christ above me,
Christ in quiet, Christ in danger,
Christ in hearts of all that love me,
Christ in mouth of friend and stranger.

I bind unto myself the name, the strong name of the Trinity;
By invocation of the same, the Three in One, and One in Three.
Of whom all nature hath creation, eternal Father, Spirit, Word:
Praise to the Lord of my salvation, salvation is of Christ the Lord. Amen.[3]

Additional Examples Commended by the Seminar
Compiled by John Mbiti

Africans and Their Names for God

In each item on this list, the name on the left (all upper case) is that of an ancient African ethnic group and language; in parentheses, the modern African nation with which they are associated; then, their name(s) for God.

ABALUYIA (Kenya): Wele, Nyasaye, Nabongo, Khakaba, Isaywa
ACHOLI (Uganda): Juok or Jok, Lubanga
ADJURU (Côte d'Ivoire): Nyam
AFUSARE (Nigeria): Daxunum
AKAMBA (Kenya): Mulungu, Ngai, Mumbi, Mwatuangi, Asa
AKAN (Ghana): Nyame, Nana Nyankopon, Onyame, Amowia, Amosu, Amaomee, Totorobonsu, Brekyirihunuade, Abommubuwafre, Nyaamanekose, Tetekwaframua, Nana, Borebore, Nyame Nwu Na Mawu[4]
ALUR (Uganda, Congo DR): Jok, Jok Rubanga, Jok Nyakaswiya, Jok Odudu, Jok Adranga, Jok Atar
AMBA (Uganda): Nyakara
AMBO (Zambia): Lesa, Cuta
ANKORE (Uganda): Ruhanga, Nyamuhanga, Omuhangi, Rugaba, Kazooba, Mukameiguru, Kazooba Nyamuhanga
ANUAK (Sudan): Juok
ARUSHA (Tanzania): Engai
ASANTE (Ghana, Côte d'Ivoire): Nyame, Onyankopon, Bore-Bore, Otumfoo, Otomankoma, Ananse Kokroko, Onyankopon Kwame
AUSHI (Zambia): Makumba
AZANDE (Sudan): Mbori or Mboli, Bapaizegino
BACHWA (Congo): Djakomba, Djabi
BACONGO (Angola): Nzambi
BAKENE (Uganda): Gasani
BAKWENA-TSWANA (Botswana): Modimo
BALESE (Congo): Katshonde, Tole, Mongo, Mbali, Londi
BALUBA (Congo): Leza, Lesa-Waba
BAMBARA (Mali): Jalang
BAMBUTI (Congo): Arebati, Epilipili, Baatsi
BAMILEKE (Cameroon): Si
BAMUM (Cameroon): Njinyi or Nui, Yorubang

BANEN (Cameroon): Hoel, Kolo, Ombang

BANYARWANDA (Rwanda): Imana, Hategekimana, Hashakimana, Habyarimana, Ndagijimana, Habimana, Bizimana, Bigirimana, Ruremakwaci

BANYORO (Uganda): Ruhanga.

BARI (Sudan): Ngun

BAROTSE (Zambia): Lesa, Nyambe

BARUNDI (Burundi): Imana, Rangicavyose, Rugiravyose, Indavyi, Rurema, Rugoba, Haragakiza, Harerimana, Rutunga, Rutangaboro, Segaba, Umusemyi, Mushoboravyose, Nyeninganyi, Rushoboravyose, Ntakimunanira, Inchanyi, Ruremabibondo, Rufashaboro, Ntirandekuva

BASA (Nigeria): Agwatana

BASOGA (Uganda): Kibumba, Kiduma, Kyaka, Nambubi, Lubanga

BASUTO (Lesotho): Molimo

BAVENDA (South Africa): Raluvhimba, Mwari

BAYA (Central African Republic): So, Zambi

BEIR (Sudan): Tummu

BEMBA (Zambia): Lesa, Mulungu, Mwandanshi, Tengenene, Katebebe, Kaleka-Misuma, Kapekape, Kalamfya-Milalo, Kanshiwabikwa, Kashawaliko, Mulopwe, Mwine-twalo, Nalusandulula, Naluntuntwe, Nalwebela, Nafukatila, Kalenga, Nakabumba, Ndubulwila

BENA (Tanzania): Mulungu

BINAWA (Nigeria): Kashiri

BIRIFOR (Ghana): We, Nawe, Wene, Yini

BONDEI (Tanzania): Mlungu

BONGO (Sudan): Loma, Hege

BORAN (Ethiopia, Kenya): Waqa

BULU (Cameroon): Mebee

BURJI-KONSO (Ethiopia): Illalei, Bambelle

CHAGGA (Tanzania): Ruwa

CHAWAI (Nigeria): Bawai

CHEWA (Malawi): Mulungu, Namalenga, Leza, Cham'njili, Mphambe, Chisumphi, Chanta, Mlengi, Mlamulili, Mcizi, Mpulumutsi, Mlezi, Wolera, Mtetezi, Muweluzi

CHOKWE (Angola): Kalunga, Zambi

CHOPI (Mozambique): Tilo

DIDINGA (Sudan): Tamukujen

DIGO (Kenya): Mulungu

DILLING (Sudan): Abradi

DINKA (Sudan): Nhialic, Acek, Jok

DOGON (Burkina Faso, Mali): Amma
DOREI (Nigeria): Nillah
DUALA (Cameroon): Loba, Owasi, Iwonde, Ebasi
DUNGI (Nigeria): Kasiri, Kashira
DURUMA (Kenya): Mulungu
EBRIE (Ivory Coast): Nyangka
EDO (Nigeria): Osanobua, Osa
EGEDE (Nigeria): Ohe
EKOI (Cameroon, Nigeria): Osawa, Nsi
ELGEYO (Kenya): Asis
EMBU (Kenya): Ngai
EWE (Benin, Ghana, Togo): Mawu
FAJULU (Sudan): Ngun
FANG (Cameroon, Gabon, Equatorial Guinea): Nzeme, Nyame
FANTI (Ghana): Nyame, Nyankopon, Twerempong
FINGO (South Africa): Qamata
FON (Benin): Mawu-Lisa
GA (Ghana): Dzemawon, Numbo
GAALIN (Sudan): Allat, Uzza, Manat
GANDA (Uganda): Katonda, Kagingo, Mukama, Ssewannaku, Ddunda, Lugaba, Ssebintu, Liisoddene, Nnyiniggulu, Kazooba, Namuginga, Ssewaunaku, Gguluddene, Namugereka
GBARI (Nigeria): Shekohi, Sheshu, Soko, Esse, Sheko
GELABA (Ethiopia): Yer
GIKUYU (Kenya): Murungu, Ngai, Mwenenyaga
GIRYAMA (Kenya): Mulungu
GISU (Uganda): Wele or Weri, Omubumbi, Wele Wehangagi
GOFA (Ethiopia): Tsuossa
GOGO (Tanzania): Mulungu
GRUNSHI (Ghana): We
GUMUZ (Ethiopia): Robboqua, Fogatza, Musa, Musa Gueza
GUSII (Kenya): Erioba (Sun)
GWERE (Uganda): Kibumba
HADYA (Ethiopia): Wa'a
HAYA (Tanzania): Ishwanga
HEHE (Tanzania): Nguluvi
HERERO (Namibia): Ndjambi Karunga, Mukuru
HOTTENTOS (South Africa): Utixo
IBIBIO (Nigeria): Abassi, Chuku
IDOMA (Nigeria): Owo, Owoico

IGBIRA (Nigeria): Hinegba, Ihinegba
IGBO (Nigeria): Chukwu, Chi, Chineke, Olisa bi n'igwé
IJAW (Nigeria): Egbesu
ILA (Zambia): Leza, Chilenga, Lubumba, Shakapanga, Namulenga, Mutalabala, Namakungwe, Muninde, Chaba, Ipaokubozha, Ushatwakwe, Shakatabwa, Mangwe, Shakemba, Kemba, Namesi, Munamazuba, Luvhunabaumba, Mukubwe, Chembwe, Munakasungwe, Chabawakaaba-ochitadiwa, Shikakunamo
INDEM (Nigeria): Osowo
INGASSANA (Ethiopia): Tel
ITSEKIRI (Nigeria): Oritse
IYALA (Nigeria): Owo
JIE (Uganda): Akuj
JUKUN (Nigeria): Shido or Chido, Ama or Ma
JUMJUM (Sudan): Dyong
KADARA (Nigeria): Onum
KAFA (Ethiopia): Yaro
KANGORO (Nigeria): Gwaza
KAIBI (Nigeria): Kashiri or Kashira
KAKWA (Sudan): Nguleso
KAMASYA (Kenya): Asis
KAONDE (Zambia): Lesa
KARAMOJA (Uganda): Akuj
KARANGA (Zimbabwe): Nyadenga
KATAB (Nigeria): Gwaza
KEMANT (Ethiopia): Sanbat
KIGA (Uganda): Ruhanga, Sebahanga, Kazoba, Rugaba, Biheko
KIPSIGIS (Kenya): Asis, Chebtalel, Cheptolel, Chebango, Ngolo
KISSI (Guinea, Liberia): Hala
KITMI (Nigeria): Kashila or Kashiri
KOMA (Ethiopia): Yere Siezi, War, Wal
KONJO (Congo, Uganda): Nyamahanga
KONKOMBA (Ghana, Togo): Omborr
KONO (Sierra Leone): Meketa, Yataa
KONSO (Ethiopia): Bamballe, Adota, Waq
KONY (Kenya): Asis
KOREKORE (Zimbabwe): Wokumusoro, Musiki, Chikara, Dzivaguru
KPE (Cameroon): Lova or Loba
KPELLE (Liberia): Yala
KRACHI (Togo): Wulbari

KUCA (Ethiopia): Tosso
KUKU (Sudan): Uletet, Ngulaitait or Nguletet
KULLO (Ethiopia): Tosa
KUBA (Congo): Nceme, Mbombo, Njambe
KUNG (Namibia): Khu, Xu, Xuba, Huwa
KURAMA (Nigeria): Ashili, Bakashili
KYIGA (Uganda): Weri
LALA (Zambia): Lesa, Mulenga, Cuuta, Lucele
LAMBA (Zambia): Lesa
LANGO (Uganda): Jok
LELE (Congo): Njambi
LENDU (Congo): Gindri
LIMBA (Sierra Leone): Kanu, Masala, Masaranka
LOBI (Côte d'Ivoire): Tangba You
LODAGAA (Ghana, Burkina Faso): Na'angmin
LOGO (Congo): Tore, Ore, Ori, Djuka
LOKOIYA (Sudan): Oicok
LOTUKO (Sudan): Ajok, Naijok
LOZI (Zambia): Nyambe
LUAPULA (Zambia): Lesa
LUGBARA (Congo, Uganda): Adroa or Adronga, Adro
LUGURU (Tanzania): Mulungu
LUIMBE (Angola): Nzambi, Kalunga
LUNDA-LUENA (Angola, Congo, Zambia) Nzambi, Kalunga, Sakatanga
LUO (Kenya): Nyasaye, Wang' Chieng', Nyakolaga, Were, Tham, Wuonwa, Wuon kwere, Wuon ji, Ja Mrima, Jan'gwono, Jahera, Nyakalaga, Janen, Wuon Ogendni, Hono, Polo, Wuon lowo, Ratego, Jalweny, Kwar ji, Rahuma, Piny k'nyal, Wuon oru, Ruodh Ruodhi, Wang' Chieng', Nyakolaga, Uworo
LUVEDU (South Africa): Khuzwane, Mwari
MAASAI (Kenya, Tanzania): En-kai, Engai, N'gai, Ai, Parsai, Emayian
MADI (Uganda): Ori, Rabanga
MAHRAKA (Sudan): Mboli
MALE (Ethiopia): Sosi
MDINGE (Guinea, Mali): Gala, Guele, Jalang
MAMVU-MANGUTU (Congo): Mai, Oti, Tore, Kundumbendu, Oto
MAO (Ethiopia): Yere, Yeretsi
MASONGO (Ethiopia): Waqaio
MATENGO (Malawi): Ciuta, Mulungu, Mlezi, Cisumphi
MEBAN (Sudan): Juong

MEKAN (Ethiopia): Tuma
MENDI (Sierra Leone): Ngewo, Leve)
MERU (Kenya): Murungu, Ngai, Mwene inya
MONDARI (Sudan): Ngun
MORU (Sudan): Lu
MOSSI (Burkina Faso): Winnam, Ouennam, Winde, Naba Zidiwinde
MURLE (Ethiopia): Tummu
NAMA (Namibia): Tsui-Goeb (Supreme Being), Cagn or Kaang, Khub, Nanub
NANDI (Kenya): Asis, Cheptalil, Chepkeliensokol or Chepkelienpokol, Chepopkoiyo, Chebonamuni
NDEBELE (Zimbabwe): Unkulunkulu, Umlimo, Mwali
NDOGO (Sudan): Mbiri, Mviri
NGOMBE (Congo): Akongo, Bilikonda, Ebangala, Ebangala-e-mokonda, Eliamokonda, EliMalima, Endandala
NGONDE (Malawi): Kyala, Mbepo Mwikemo, Ndolombwike, Kamanyimanyi, Mpoki
NGONI (Malawi): Unkurukuru, Utixo, Inkosi, Umkulunqango, Uluhlanga, Umkulu Kakulu, Umnikaze we zinto zonke
NKUM (Nigeria): Oshowo, Ebutokpabi
NKUNDO (Congo): Djakomba
NSÓ (Cameroon): Nyuỳ
NUBA (Sudan) Kalo, Elo, Bel, Bel Epti, Kando, Kwarak, Masala, Elem
NUER (Sudan): Kwoth
NUPE (Nigeria): Soko
NYAKYUSA (Tanzania): Kyala, Tenende, Nkurumuke, Chata Kyaubiri, Kalesi, Ndorombwike, Mperi
NYANJA (Zambia, Malawi): Mulungu, Cuata, Leza, Mphamba, Cisumphi, Cimjili Namalenga or Nyamalenga or Mlengi
OKIET (Kenya): Asis
OROMO (Ethiopia, Kenya): Waqa
ORRI (Nigeria): Lokpata
OVIMBUNDU (Angola): Suku, Usovoli
PARE (Tanzania): Kyumbi, Mrungu, Izuva
PITI (Nigeria): Ure
POKOMO (Kenya): Muungu
POKOT (Kenya): Tororut, Ilat
PONDO (South Africa): uDali, uMenzi, uTixo
PYGMY (Congo): Kmvoum
PYEM (Nigeria): Wudidi

RABAI (Kenya): Mulungu
RISHUWA (Nigeria): Kashiri, Kasiri
RUKUBA (Nigeria): Katakuru
RUMAIYA (Nigeria): Kashillo, Kashira
SAFWA (Tanzania): Nguruvi
SONATA (Congo): Nja
SAN (Botswana, Namibia): Urezhwa
SANDAWE (Tanzania): Waronge, Murungu
SANGAMA (Ethiopia): Zabi
SEBEI (Uganda): Oiki, Oinotet
SERER (Gambia, Senegal): Rog
SHERBRO-BULLOM-KRIM (Sierra Leone): Hobatoke
SHILLUK (Sudan): Juok
SHONA (Zimbabwe): Mwari, Nyadenga, Wokumusoro, Gore, Runji, Chipindikure, Chirozva-mauya Chirazamauya, Sagomakoma, Musiki, Muvumbi, Marure, Musikavanhu, Dzivaguru, Chidziva, Mutangakugara, Muwanikwa, Mupavose, Wemumbepo, Muponesi, Muyaradzi, Muratidzi
SIDAMO (Ethiopia): Magano
SONGHAY (Nigeria): Yerkoy
SONJO (Tanzania): Mugwe, Riob
SOTHO (Lesotho): Molimo, Molimo o matle
SRUBU (Nigeria): Kasiri, Kahiri
SUKUMA-NYAMWEZI (Tanzania): Mulungu, Mungu, Seba, Kube, Kube-Nyangasa, Limi, Linyabangwe, Liwelelo, Ng'wenekili, Ling'wenekili, Likubala
SURI-SUMMA (Ethiopia): Tuma
SWAZI (Swaziland): Mkulumncandi, Umkhulumncandi, Inkosatana, Umvelingquangi
TALLENZI (Ghana, Burkina Faso): We, Wene, Nawe, Nabwe
TEITA (Kenya): Mlungu
TEMBU (South Africa): uTixo
TEMNE (Sierra Leone): Kuru, Kurumasaba
TENDA (Guinea): Hounounga
TESO (Uganda): Akuj, Apap, Edeke, Lokasuban
TEUSO (Uganda): Didikwari, Nakwit
THONGS (South Africa, Mozambique): Tilo, Hosi, Xikwembu
TIKAR (Cameroon): Nyooiy
TIV (Nigeria): Aondo
TLHAPING (South Africa): Modimo

TONGA (Malawi, Zambia): Tilo, Chiuta or Ciuta, Leza, Mlengi, Chata, Nyangoi, Wamu yaya, Wanthazizose, Mkana Nyifwa, Kajeti, Mtaski, Msungi, Mlezi, Mlengavuwa, Mnanda, Mananda, Mangazi
TOPOSA (Sudan): Nakwuge
TORO (Uganda): Nkya, Ruhanga, Kagaba, Nyamuhanga
TSWANA (Botswana, South Africa): Modimo
TUMBUKA (Malawi): Chiuta, Mulengi, Leza, Mwati, Mweni-Nkongono, Kajilengi, Wamtatakuya, Cinyetenyete, Mweneco, Mupi, Cilera-balanda, Karonga wa mabanja, Cimbatakwinya, Kamphanda, Kamanyimanyi, Wamalumya
TURKANA (Kenya): Akuj
TURU (Tanzania): Murungu, Matunda
TWI (Benin, Ghana): Onyankopon
UDHUK (Ethiopia): Arumgimis
URHOBO-ISOKO (Nigeria): Oghene, Oghenukpabe
VAI (Liberia): Kamba
VENDA (South Africa): Nwali
VILI (Congo): Nzambi Mpungu
VUGUSU (Kenya): Wele
WALAMO (Ethiopia): Tosa
XAM (South Africa): Kaang, Kaggen, Huwu or Huwe
XHOSA (South Africa): uThixo, uDali (Maker, Creator), uMenzi, uHlanga, Qamata
YACHI (Nigeria): Phahia
YAKO (Nigeria): Ubasi
YAO (Malawi, Mozambique): Mulungu
YORUBA (Nigeria): Olodumare, Olorun, Olofin-Orun
ZALA (Ethiopia): Taosa
ZINZA (Tanzania): Isewahanga, Kazoba, Rugaba
ZULU (South Africa): Unkulunkulu, Inkosi, uDumakade, uGobungqongqo, uGuqabadele, uKqili, uMabonga-kutuk-izizwe-zonke, uSomoganiso, uZivelele.[5]

Matthew Bridges (1800–94)

Crown Him with Many Crowns

Crown him with many crowns,
the Lamb upon his throne;

while Heaven's eternal anthem drowns
all music but its own!
Awake, my soul, and sing
of him who died to be
your Savior and your matchless King
through all eternity.

Crown him the Lord of Life
triumphant from the grave,
who rose victorious from the strife
for those he came to save:
his glories now we sing
who died and rose on high;
he died eternal life to bring
and lives that death may die.

Crown him the Son of God
before the worlds began;
and you who tread where he has trod,
crown him the Son of Man,
who every grief has known
that wrings the human breast,
and takes and bears them for his own,
that all in him may rest.

Crown him the Lord of Love,
who shows his hands and side—
those wounds yet visible above
in beauty glorified.
No angel in the sky
can fully bear that sight,
but downward bends his burning eye
at mysteries so bright.

Crown him the Lord of Years,
the Potentate of Time,
Creator of the rolling spheres
in majesty sublime:
all hail, Redeemer, hail,
for you have died for me;

your praise shall never, never fail
through all eternity![6]

Caroline Maria Noel (1817–77)

At the Name of Jesus, Every Knee Shall Bow

At the name of Jesus ev'ry knee shall bow,
ev'ry tongue confess him King of glory now;
'tis the Father's pleasure we should call him Lord,
who from the beginning was the mighty Word.

At his voice creation sprang at once to sight,
all the angel faces, all the hosts of light,
cherubim in heaven, stars upon their way,
all the heav'nly orders in their great array.

Humbled for a season to receive a name
from the lips of sinners unto whom he came,
faithfully he bore it spotless to the last,
brought it back victorious when from death he passed;

Bore it up triumphant with its human light,
thro' all ranks of creatures to the central height,
to the throne of Godhead, to the Father's breast,
filled it with the glory of that perfect rest.

In your hearts enthrone him; there let him subdue
all that is not holy, all that is not true;
crown him as your captain in temptation's hour;
let his will enfold you in its light and pow'r.

Christians, this Lord Jesus shall return again
in his Father's glory, with his angel train;
for all wreaths of empire meet upon his brow,
and our hearts confess him King of glory now.[7]

Notes

1. Building Bridges Seminar 2021 participants were encouraged to listen to these recordings of *The God of Abraham Praise*: https://www.youtube.com/watch?v=_k0WbiQXiHw; https://www.youtube.com/watch?v=vzQMrjnAZXc.

2. Building Bridges Seminar 2021 participants were encouraged to listen to these recordings of *The Advent Antiphons:* https://www.youtube.com/watch?v=8ngcQDQfhlA&list=PLM_BPPe3btzjYhja2ufL8ffepQLsk3KQ8; https://www.youtube.com/watch?v=hhK_SjfMDX4. See also the well-known carol based on the O Antiphons: *O Come, O Come, Emmanuel!* Text only: https://hymnary.org/text/o_come_o_come_emmanuel_and_ransom; performance: https://www.youtube.com/watch?v=ikEtkfRSUsU.

3. Here the text is sung to the tune *St. Patrick's Breastplate* by the Choir of Keble College: https://www.youtube.com/watch?v=q5Hin4swdKg. For many years this hymn was sung at the General Theological Seminary of the Episcopal Church (New York City) during the September matriculation ceremony as new students were called individually to sign the enrollment book. Here it is in that context, with Professor David Hurd, organist: http://news.gts.edu/2013/09/st-patricks-breastplate-recording-from-gts-matriculation-2002/?fbclid=IwAR1Oc6fW-xuuwfbjJRbWcWiWluDr4X19ncfZRYSnWJKraU3-mI2v6xDVx3U.

4. Mbiti explains: *Nyame nwu na mawu* (loosely translated, "God does not die, so I cannot die") is the Akan *adinkra*, or proverb, that symbolizes the continuity of the human spirit in temporal affairs. This idea envisions death as a transition between physical and immaterial states of being, with the dead remaining consequential players in the societies in which they lived.

5. This list of 631 names of God in 102 African languages, as found in thirty African countries, is included in John S. Mbiti, *Concepts of God in Africa* (London: SPCK, 1970). For many years this list was also made available by Maryknoll Language Institute (Musoko, Tanzania) as *African Names, Titles, Images, Descriptions, and Attributes of God.* It is now promulgated on several websites.

6. The text is sung here to the tune *Diademata*: https://www.youtube.com/watch?v=If-svStcvS8.

7. The daughter of an Anglican clergyman, Caroline Maria Noel (1817–77) wrote devotional poetry from age seventeen to twenty. Having become an invalid at age thirty-five, she resumed that practice at age forty as a means of solace. Her collected devotional poetry was published as *The Name of Jesus and Other Verses for the Sick and Lonely* in 1861, and as a similarly titled larger volume in 1870. The 1870 volume includes "At the Name of Jesus, Ev'ry Knee Shall Bow," a processional hymn for the Feast of the Ascension that is based on Philippians 2:5–11. See Nancy Roth, *Awake My Soul! Meditating on Hymns for Year B* (New York: Church Publishing, 1999), 145–46. Here the poem is sung to the tune *Camberwell* by the Salisbury Cathedral Choir (United Kingdom): https://www.youtube.com/watch?v=KV6cHI4mZvE; here, to the tune *Evelyns* by the Chapel Choir of Marlborough College: https://www.youtube.com/watch?v=nkkL0eWq1Uw; and here to the majestic tune *King's Weston* (composed by Ralph Vaughan Williams specifically for this text) by the Cardiff (Wales) Festival Choir: https://www.youtube.com/watch?v=S2RjIeFnKlY.

11

A Matter of Theurgy

The Impact of Naming God in Muslim Devotional Practice

Reza Shah-Kazemi

In making the transition from studying the principle of naming God in scripture and theology to the spiritual discipline of naming God in devotional practice, the key idea to be kept in mind is that of the theurgic impact of the Name or Names of God. By *theurgy* we mean something akin to the concept of *tajallī*, the self-disclosure or theophanic manifestation of God. This divine self-disclosure both reveals and attracts: it is at once energetically radiant revelation and powerfully magnetic attraction. As Gregory Shaw tells us in his important book on the Syrian Neoplatonist philosopher Iamblichus, theurgy (*theourgia*) is "God-work"—as opposed to theology, which is "God-talk."[1]

The ancient Greeks, together with the ancient Egyptians, Chaldeans, and Mesopotamians, understood that the efficacy of theurgic praxis resides in the fact that the gods themselves are not only naming themselves but also performing the inner work of spiritual transformation.[2] This, notwithstanding the fact that human beings are performing the outward acts of invocation, meditation, incantation, contemplation, and so forth. The divine act of naming itself precedes the human practice of invocation, both with respect to ontological causality and to mystical grace. Imam ʿAlī (cousin and son-in-law of the Prophet, the most important spiritual guide in the Islamic tradition after the Prophet himself) summarizes this principle in the following statement about the devotional practice of the invocation: "The invocation emanates first from the Invoked (al-Madhkūr), and secondly from the invoker (*al-dhākir*)."[3]

The idea being intimated here is graphically expressed by Rumi in his *Mathnawi*, book 3. Rumi tells a story of a man who becomes dejected after the devil's insinuation that his perpetual invocation of God is fruitless, as God has not once answered him; he is then told by al-Khidr that God replies to him as follows:

> That "Allah" of thine is My "Here am I," and that supplication and grief and ardour of thine is My messenger (to thee). Thy shifts and attempts to find a means (of gaining access to Me) were (in reality) My drawing (thee towards Me), and released thy feet (from the bonds of worldliness). Thy fear and love are the noose to catch My favor: beneath every "O Lord" (of thine) is many a "Here am I" (from Me).[4]

The very fact of calling upon God's Name is the result of, and a response to, a preceding call from God to man. At first blush it appears that God responds with grace to man's call to Him. Indeed, the Qur'an tells us: "And when My servants ask thee about Me, verily I am near. I answer the prayer of the pray-er when he prays to Me" (Q. 2:186).[5]

The word *when* (*idhā*) here is important. We could almost translate it in this context as follows: "I answer the prayer of the pray-er *as* He prays to Me." A mysterious coincidence of call and response is being hinted at: the call and the response are two sides of the same coin, a bi-unity, the very fact of human invocation apparently generating but actually constituting, in and of itself, the corresponding (and not just "responding") divine grace.

The principle that the divine call to humanity both ontologically and temporally precedes humanity's call to God is indicated in the rest of the verse just cited: "So let them answer Me, and believe in Me, that they might be rightly guided" (Q. 2:186). From the Sufi perspective, the perpetual call of God to man is the Qur'anic question: "Am I not your Lord" (7:172), the question put to all human beings prior to their being born on earth; it is the divine command, the *fiat, be, kun!* It is the naming of humanity, our "re-membering," our being invoked and thereby brought into existence by God, according to the following verse: "Has there come upon man any moment in time when he was not a thing remembered (*shay'an madhkūran*)?" (Q. 76:1). Our being a "thing remembered" is identical to our existentiation; our nonexistence is equivalent to our being "not remembered." Humankind is subject to perpetual re-creation by divine re-membering, being "named," being invoked. Human invocation is thus a conscious and active participation in his own perpetual re-creation by divine invocation/re-membering. To go back to Rumi's story: our invocation of God is His re-creation of us.

Ibn ʿAṭāʾillāh al-Iskandarī

The relationship between invocation and re-creation takes us to the aphorisms of the thirteenth century Egyptian saint Ibn ʿAṭāʾillāh al-Iskandarī. He says:

> Do not abandon the invocation because you do not feel the Presence of God therein. For your forgetfulness of the invocation of him is worse than your forgetfulness in the invocation of Him. Perhaps He will take you from an invocation with forgetfulness (*ghafla*) to one with vigilance (*yaqaẓa*), and from one with vigilance to one with the Presence of God (*ḥuḍūr*), and from one with the Presence of God to one wherein everything but the Invoked (*al Madhkhūr*) is absent. "And that is not difficult for God" (Q. 35:17).[6]

The Name of God contains the theurgic authority, *sulṭān*, because it is revealed by God Himself, in contrast to "names which you yourself have named, you and your forefathers before you" (Q. 12:40). It is this theurgic authority that accounts for the incommensurable grace that is, as it were, lying latent within the practice of the invocation of the Name of God. This is a grace that is capable to taking one all the way from heedlessness to *fanāʾ* (extinction in the Divine Presence) and *baqāʾ* (subsistence through that Presence). This is tantamount to a re-creation of the very substance of the soul, as the Qurʾanic words cited elliptically by Ibn ʿAṭāʾillāh at the end of this aphorism indicate. For the verse cited—"And that is not difficult for God" (Q. 35:17)—comes after these two verses: "O mankind, ye are the poor unto God, and God, He is the Rich, the Praiseworthy. If He will, He could remove you and replace you with a new creation (*khalq jadīd*)" (Q. 35:15–16).

It is only in the measure of one's poverty (*faqr*, being a *faqīr*, pl. *fuqarāʾ*) that one is fully receptive to this transformative power. When our invocation of the Divine Name is accompanied by our awareness that we are nothing before God, we are opening ourselves up to the transformative power inherent in the Name, this power which is in essence nothing other than the Named, for, according to the following maxim—a veritable touchstone of Sufi mystical praxis: "the Name is the Named" (*al-ism huwaʾl-musammā*).

This takes us to the second extract from Ibn ʿAṭāʾillāh, in which he says: "Invoking the letters of God's Name without presence of mind is invocation of the tongue; invoking with presence of mind is invocation of the heart; and invoking with an absence of self-awareness because of absorption in the Invoked is the invocation of the Self. This is the hidden invocation!"[7] The invocation of the Name removes the rust from the heart, according to a seminal saying of the Prophet. For everything there is a polish; and the polish of the hearts is *dhikru'Llāh*. The rust over the heart is not just heedlessness of God, it is that congenital egotism which self-awareness is. If the essential being of man is engendered by the *remembrance* that God has of him; and if the essence of man's devotion to God is expressed by the heartfelt invocation of the Divine Name, then the ultimate fruit of human invocation is the extinction of the limitations of human consciousness in the essence of divine reality.

This is evident in one of the most revealing of Imam ʿAlī's statements about the invocation. Here he contrasts what he calls a "perfect remembrance" (*dhikran kāmilan*) with the "spiritual reality" of remembrance (*ḥaqīqatu' l-dhikr*); the first pertains to the human aspect of remembrance, the second, to its divine mystery; the first expressing sincerity and concentration, the second intimating the transcendence of all human virtues and faculties that comes about through the grace of self-effacement (*fanāʾ*). Hence he says:

> Do not remember God absent-mindedly, nor forget Him in distraction; rather, remember Him with perfect remembrance, a remembrance in which your heart and tongue are in harmony, and what is inwardly hidden within you conforms with what you outwardly manifest. But you will not remember God according to the true reality of the remembrance until you forget your self in your remembrance (*ḥattā tansā nafsaka fī dhikrika*).[8]

There is a radical incommensurability between the human practice of the invocation and its consummation in the "reality" of the invocation. The invoker's "forgetting" of his soul in the "remembrance" of God implies the complete extinction of specifically human consciousness—that is, consciousness insofar as it is limited by the boundaries of the individual human being—and its reabsorption into the source of consciousness. This perspective also resonates with the theurgic traditions referred to earlier. According to Gregory Shaw: "Theurgic rites transformed the soul from being its own idol, in an inverted attitude of self-interest, into an icon of the divine, with its very corporeality changed into a vehicle of transcendence."[9]

To conclude, let us consider how this naming of God sounds in practice. One might engage in a session of *dhikr*. One might recite a litany of God's Names. There is, of course, a famous litany of the Ninety-Nine Names. However, there is also a litany of Names of God in Imam ʿAlī's supplication titled *al-Mashlūl* (The ailing person). Properly recited, it conveys something of the theurgic quality of the invocation of the Names of God that countless Muslims throughout history have found irresistibly transformative.[10]

Let us note that God's Names are not restricted to those that are mentioned in the Qur'anic revelation, or those known as the "Ninety-Nine Names." Imam ʿAlī calls upon God by means of every Name "by which God has named Himself," in any of His scriptural revelations, and even by those Names that He has kept hidden in His own Essence. We are thus invited to participate in a vision, or an intuition, of the mystery of the "names" or "traces" of those qualities of ultimate reality that transcend human thought and language. These qualities of the Transcendent can be intuited as so many musical "notes" within the soundless harmony of the ineffable Divine Essence, notes that are beyond sensorial sound but that are nonetheless the divine archetypes of all harmony, beauty, and holiness in the cosmos. Every single phenomenon in existence is thus a "name" of the Nameless, "sung" by the Singer in a revelation at once reverberating and reintegrating.

Notes

1. Gregory Shaw, *Theurgy and the Soul: The Neoplatonism of Iamblichus* (University Park: Pennsylvania State University Press, 1995), 4–5.

2. See Algis Uzdavinys, *Philosophy and Theurgy in Late Antiquity* (San Rafael, CA: Sophi Perennis, 2010); and *Philosophy as a Rite of Rebirth: From Ancient Egypt to Neoplatonism* (Westbury, Wiltshire, UK: Prometheus Trust, 2008).

3. No. 2098 in Anṣārī, ed., *Ghurar al-ḥikam* (Publisher), 135. *Ghurar al-Hikam wa Durar al-Kalim* (exalted aphorisms and pearls of speech) is a compilation by Qadhi Nasih Al-Deen Abu al-Fath Abd al-Wahid Ibn Muhammad al-Tamimi al-Amudi of some 10,760 assertions and aphorisms attributed to Imam ʿAlī ibn Abi Talib.

4. Reynold A. Nicholson, trans., *The Mathnawi of Jalaluddin Rumi*, book 3 (London: Luzac & Co., 1930), lines 195–202.

5. *The Study Quran* renders the second clause of Q. 2:186 thus: "I answer the call of the caller when he calls Me." Seyyed Hossein Nasr, et al., *The Study Quran* (New York: HarperOne, 2015), 82.

6. Victor Danner, trans., *Ibn ʿAṭāʾillāh's Sufi Aphorisms* (Leiden: E. J. Brill, 1973), 32.

7. Ibn ʿAṭāʾillāh al-Iskandarī, *The Key to Salvation: A Sufi Manual of Invocation*, trans. Mary Ann Khoury Danner (Cambridge: Islamic Texts Society, 1996; repr. 2012), 51.

8. No. 7524 in Anṣārī, ed., *Ghurar*, 621, x. For further discussion of this text, see Reza Shah-Kazemi, *Justice and Remembrance: Introducing the Spirituality of Imam Ali* (London: I.B. Tauris, 2007), 162–70. It is interesting to note that several Sufi exegetes use, implicitly, the principle enunciated here by the Imam as the key for explaining the verse in the Sūrat al-Kahf apparently remonstrating with the Prophet: "Remember your Lord when you have forgotten" (Q. 18:24).

9. Gregory Shaw, "Theurgy: Rituals of Unification in the Neoplatonism of Iamblichus," in *Traditio* 49 (1985): 25; cited by Algis Uždavinys, "Putting on the Form of the Gods: Sacramental Theurgy in Neoplatonism," in *Sacred Web* 5 (Summer 2000): 113.

10. For the text of this litany, other items mentioned in this chapter, and related Islamic devotional texts, see the next chapter in the present volume.

12

Muslim Devotional Literature on Naming God

Selections for Dialogue

Ahmad ibn Muhammad ibn ʿAṭāʾillāh

Aphorism No. 47 from Kitāb al-Ḥikam (The Book of Wisdom)

Do not abandon the invocation (*al-dhikr*) because you do not feel the Presence (*ḥuḍūr*) of God therein. For your forgetfulness of the invocation of him is worse than your forgetfulness in the invocation of Him. Perhaps He will take you from an invocation with forgetfulness (*ghafla*) to one with vigilance (*yaqaẓa*), and from one with vigilance to one with the Presence of God, and from one with the Presence of God to one wherein everything but the Invoked (*al-Madhkhūr*) is absent. "And that is not difficult for God."[1]

Ibn ʿAṭāʾillāh al-Iskandarī

Passages from Miftāḥ al-Falāḥ wa Misbāḥ al-Arwāḥ (The Key to Salvation and the Lamp of Souls)

Introduction: On the Nature of Remembrance and Its Explanation

Remembrance of God is liberation from ignorance and forgetfulness through the permanent presence of the heart with the Truth. It has been said that it is the repetition of the Name of the Invoked by the heart and the tongue. It is alike whether it is God who is remembered, or one of His attributes, or one of His commandments, or one for His deeds, or whether one draws a conclusion based on any one of these. . . .[2]

Note: Invoking the letters of God's Name without presence of mind is invocation of the tongue; invoking with presence of mind is invocation of the heart; and invoking with an absence of self-awareness because of absorption in the Invoked is the invocation of the Self—this is the hidden invocation! . . .[3]

On the Benefits of the Invocations Used by the Novice Traveling the Path

Know that the Most Beautiful Names (al-Asmāʾ al-Ḥusnā) of God are a medicine for the maladies of the heart and the sicknesses of those travelling to the presence of the Divine Knower of the Invisible World. A remedy is not to be used except for illnesses which that particular Name benefits. For example, where the name "the Giver" (al-Muʿṭi) is beneficial for a particular illness of the heart, a Name which is not salutary for that situation is not prescribed, and so forth.

The rule is that whosoever uses an invocation, and that invocation has an intelligible meaning, the influence of that meaning attaches itself to his heart, followed by the corollary significations of the meaning, until the invoker is characterized by those qualities. Thus so unless the Name be one of the Names of vengeance in which case fear clings to the heart of the invoker; and if inspiration comes to him, it is from the world of Majesty (al-Jalāl).

His Name (exalted be He!) "the Truthful" (aṣ-Ṣādiq): Its invocation bestows on the one who is veiled truthfulness (*ṣidq*) of tongue; of the Sufi adherent, truthfulness of heart; and on the Gnostic, realization.

His Name (exalted be He!) "the Guide" (al-Hādī): It is salutary during spiritual retreat (*khalwah*). It is beneficial against the state of dispersion and distraction, and eliminates them. Whosoever seeks the help of God but does not see the visible signs of assistance forthcoming, then let him know that his continually asking for God is what is sought from him.

His Name (exalted be He!) "the Resurrector" (al-Bāʿith): Those who are forgetful invoked it; but those who are possessed of extinction do not invoke it.

His Name (exalted be He!) "the Pardoner (al-ʿAfuw): It is appropriate for common people to invoke it, because it improves them; but its invocation is not the concern of travelers on the path to God, because the remembrance of sin is implicit therein. The invocation of the initiates does not contain the remembrance of sin, nor for that matter, the remembrance of good deeds.

However, when the common people invoke the Name, it ameliorates their spiritual state.

His Name (exalted be He!) "the Protector" (al-Mawlā): He is the Victor and the Master. Only servants having special affinity with this Name invoke it. If others who are spiritually above them invoke the Name, it has a different significance.

His Name (exalted be He!) "the One Who Beautifies" (al-Muḥsin): It is appropriate for the generality of believers when attainment of the station of trust in God is desired for them. Invoking this Name necessitates intimacy with God and hastens spiritual insight. With it the novice is treated against the awesome fear of the world of Majesty (al-Jalāl).

His Name (exalted be He!) "the All-Knowing" (al-ʿAllām): Its invocation arouses one from forgetfulness and makes the heart be present with the Lord. It teaches proper conduct accompanied with vigilance. Amongst the devotees of Beauty (al-Jamāl), the Name confers upon the heart intimacy (*uns*) with God; and amongst the devotees of Majesty (al-Jalāl), the Name renews fear and awe in the heart.

His Name (exalted be He!) "the Forgiver" (al-Ghāfir): It is assigned for the generality of disciples who fear punishment of sin. As for those who are worthy of the Divine Presence, remembrance of the forgiveness of sins causes alienation in them. Likewise the remembrance of good deeds causes thoughtlessness, generating in the soul a notion somewhat as if it had done God a favor in serving Him through acts of obedience or in remembering the harm of evil deeds.

His Name (exalted be He!) "the Firm" (al-Matīin): It means hard. This name is harmful to those in seclusion (*khalwah*); but it is beneficial to those who mock religion and returns them, throughout the duration of their remembrance of it, to submissiveness and obedience.

His Name (exalted be He!) "the Rich" (al-Ghanī): Invoking it is beneficial to those who seek disengagement from worldly things but are unable to do so alone.

His Name (exalted be He!) "the Reckoner" (al-Ḥasib): If the invoker of it is infatuated with the activities of gaining a livelihood, he emerges from them toward disengagement because of contentment with the Reckoner, that is, the Sufficient (al-Kāfī).

His Name (exalted be He!) "the Nourisher" (al-Muqit): Invoking it helps in disengaging oneself from the cares of gaining a living and bestows trust in God.

His Name (exalted be He!) "the Possessor of Majesty" (Dhu'l-Jalal): It is good during retreat for those who are forgetful.

His Name (exalted be He!) "the Creator" (al-Khaliq): It is among the Names invoked by the people who have the station of religious devotion (*'ibādah*) by virtue of conjoining beneficial knowledge with pious deeds. It is not suitable to be taught to those with a unique receptivity, for it estranges them from gnosis and draws them toward mental reckoning.

His Name (exalted be He!) "the Fashioner" (al-Muṣawwir): It is among the invocations of pious servants.

His Name (exalted be He!) "the Knower" (al-'Ālim): It is among the invocations of pious servants. It is good for the beginners among those travelling the path, for there is a reminder of vigilance in it; and through it fear and hope are obtained.

His Name (exalted be He!) "the Counter" (al-Muḥṣīi): It is among the invocations of pious servants.

His Name (exalted be He!) "the Watcher" (ar-Raqīb): When those who are forgetful invoke it, they awaken from their slumber. When the wakeful invoke it, they remain in a wakeful state. If pious worshippers invoke it, they are freed of hypocrisy. Neither those who are in control of their actions nor the Gnostics need to invoke it; nor does it have any relationship with those who are utterly extinguished in the Goal, because they have gone beyond the Names. . . .

Section [One]

His Name (exalted be He!) "the Trustworthy" (al-Wafi): It is the invocation of the intermediates on the path. Invoking it during retreat confers acceptance to the ultimate content of one's receptivity.

His Name (exalted be He!) "the Thankful" (al-Shakir): That is, the One Who is grateful to His pious servant for his deed, namely, He commends him for it. It bestows on the adepts of the invocation the station of love if they are Sufis, the station of extinction if they are Gnostics, and the station of centrality (*quṭbiyyah*) and eminence if they are of those who have reached the end. It is a holy presence surrounded by intimacy with God, and in retreat has far-reaching effects.

His Name (exalted be He!) "the Glorious" (al-Majīd): It is not used in retreat by novices, whereas it is incumbent upon intermediates to invoke it when the Truth manifests itself to them by descending to the level of "the presence of limitations" (*taqyīd*). Verily, invoking *al-Majīd* removes all forms.

His Name (exalted be He!) "the Loving" (al-Wadūd): He is Loving towards all Creation. When adepts invoke it, they achieve intimacy and love.

His Name (exalted be He!) "the Benefactor" (al-Mannān): Its invocation in retreat is very beneficial to those who have quit the pleasures of the ego, but it is harmful to those whose desires of the self remain.

His Name (exalted be He!) "the Affectionate" (al-Hannān): Its invocation in retreat strengthens intimacy until it takes its practitioner to love.

His Name (exalted be He!) "the Benign" (al-Barr): It bestows intimacy and hastens partial insight, but not union.

His Name (exalted be He!) "the Outward" (aẓ-Ẓāhir): Invoking it is beneficial during a very difficult journey.

His Name (exalted be He!) "the Cleaver" (al-Fāliq): Its invocation during a retreat profoundly benefits the renouncer and hastens the coming of illumination upon him when accompanied by the name "the Self-Subsistent" (al-Qayyūm) or "the Living" (al-Ḥayy); but it slows down illumination if "There is no divinity but God" (*Lā ilāha illa'llāh*) is invoked with it.

His Name (exalted be He!) "the Gracious" (al-Latīf): It carries with it the all-encompassing meaning of mercifulness. Invoking it during retreat benefits those who are opaque in nature and makes them more refined. It benefits the contemplatives: it strengthens the contemplation of those who were previously weak.

His Name (exalted be He!) "the Light" (an-Nūr): It is quick to bestow light and insight on those in retreat, because it does so by degrees. Rarely does it give total illumination.

His Name (exalted be He!) "the Inheritor" (al-Wārith): It is appropriate for Gnostics and attracts them towards absolute extinction in God: it is the station that ends the path.

His Name (exalted be He!) "the Giver" (al-Muʿṭī): Of all the Names invoked in retreat, it is the one most likely to bring about illumination, albeit a weak one.

His Name (exalted be He!) "the Superior" (al-Fāʾiq): The Gnostics invoke it, but not the novices.

His Name (exalted be He!) "the Grateful" (ash-Shakūr): Its invocation is a characteristic of the elite who have achieved union.

His Name (exalted be He!) "the Almighty" (Dhu'ṭ-Ṭawl): Among God's graces to us are submission (*islām*), then faith (*imān*) then virtue (*iḥsān*), then peace, then uprightness, then the freedom of conduct, then gnosis, then comprehension, then realization by degrees, and then the function of vicegerent (*khilāfah*). This invocation hastens illumination. Likewise His Names "the Opener" (al-Fattāḥ) and "the First" (al-Awwal) hasten illumination.

His Name (exalted be He!) "the Dominating" (al-Jabbār): It is conferred in retreat upon whosoever is overcome by a state and it is feared that the expansion (*basṭ*) which initiates find radiating from the Name "the Expander" (*al-Bāsiṭ*) will overwhelm him. When someone whose substance is mixed with expansion invokes it, contraction (*qabḍ*) comes upon him, and thus he becomes equilibriated in treading the path.

His Name (exalted be He!) "the Proud" (al-Mutakabbir): It is invoked in retreat and elsewhere to bring reverential fear back to the one who has been overcome by expansion.

His Name (exalted be He!) "the Able" (al-Qādir): The fruit of its invocation is that it benefits those who consider miracles (*kharq al-ʿawāʾid*) as far-fetched. So when one of them invokes the Name in his retreat, his inner being is given the grace to see their validity to a certain extent.

His Name (exalted be He!) "the Judge" (al-Qāḍī): That is, He whose judgment is obeyed. Whosoever has hesitated in matters out of ignorance and invokes this Name, God decrees for him the contemplation of Truth in his inner being.

His Name (exalted be He!) "the Strong" (al-Qawī): Its invocation benefits those who become sick during retreat or forget or become too weak to invoke or become dispersed. Truly, it unites: its virtue lies in its belonging by right to the path of kings and great men inasmuch as when they invoke it, the Name unites them in comformity with the Truth.

His Name (exalted be He!) "the Guardian" (al-Ḥafīẓ): Its characteristic is the preservation of a state. Whoever fears deception invokes it.

His Name (exalted be He!) "the Honoured" (al-Mukarram): The shaykh should order the novice to use it when the latter has a low opinion of himself and his intimacy with God is nonexistent because of his asking for forgiveness.

His Name (exalted be He!) "the Planner" (al-Mudabbir): Invoking it is not good for the traveler on the path except when the shaykh fears that the process of unification (*tawḥīd*) will overcome him.

His Name (exalted be He!) "the Great" (al-Kabīr): The shaykh should instruct the disciple to invoke it when the manifestation of nearness to God overcomes him and when the shaykh fears that the disciple will be distraught by it.

His Name (exalted be He!) "The Exalted" (al-Mutaʿālī): Like the name "the Great" (al- Kabīr), it benefits whoever is overcome by nearness to God and is beside himself. When he invokes the Name, he returns to his senses.

Section [Two]

His Name (exalted be He!) "the Potent" (al-Muqtadir): Its meaning is "the Able" (al- Qādir). He whom the shaykh wishes to manifest charismatic phenomena (*karamāt*) without union invokes this Name.

His Name (exalted be He!) "the Efficacious" (al-Fa'al): Its invocation benefits whoever desires to produce effects and charismatic phenomena.

His Name (exalted be He!) "the Reliable" (al-Wāthiq): The shaykh should give it as an invocation to whosoever he fears will be unreceptive, which would veil illumination from him.

His Name (exalted be He!) "the Restorer" (al-Mu'īd): The shaykh should assign it to whosoever he wishes to veil whenever the shaykh fears for him that illumination will make him unbalanced.

His Name (exalted be He!) "the Advancer" (al-Muqaddim): The shaykh should assign it to those who tum away from the wisdom of the Wise; hence, it brings them back to Him.

His Name (exalted be He!) "the Inward" (al-Bāṭin): It is invoked by whoever is overcome by "outward illumination," and mental confusion is feared for him. The shaykh should give it to whoever is overcome by a feeling of nearness to God to the point where he might almost become unbalanced.

His Name (exalted be He!) "the Most Holy" (al-Quddūs): The shaykh should order that it be invoked by those who are subjected in retreat to the doubts of the anthropomorphists and those who compare things with God, or those who have a similar creed. So let them avail themselves of this Name by invoking it much! But the shaykh should not order that it be invoked by any others, especially by those whose creed is Ashᶜarī, since it would make illumination impossible for them. Instead the shaykh should give them, in exchange for this Name, the Names "the Near" (al-Qarīb), "the Watcher" (al-Raqīb), "the Loving" (al-Wadūd), and the likes of these Names.

His Name (exalted be He!) "the Examiner" (al-Mumtaḥin): The shaykhs use its signification: it makes their disciples fit for guidance, so that the shaykhs can test thereby their disciples' predispositions in order to find out which way they should proceed with their disciples toward God Most High. But they should not assign this Name in retreat except to someone who has suffered a misfortune, so that it reminds him of his Lord. . . .[4]

Jalaluddin Rumi

Mathnawi, Book 3

Showing that the supplicant's invocation of God is essentially the same thing as God's response to him.

One night a certain man was crying "Allah!" till his lips were growing sweet with praise of Him. The Devil said, "Prithee, O garrulous one, where is the (response) ‘Here am I’ to all this ‘Allah’? Not a single response is coming from the Throne: how long will you cry ‘Allah’ with grim face?”

The man became broken-hearted and laid down his head (to sleep): in a dream he saw Khadir amidst the verdure. Khadir said, “Hark, you have held back from praising God: how is it that you repent of having called unto Him?”

The man said, “No ‘Here am I’ is coming to me in response, hence I fear that I may be (a reprobate who is) driven away from the Door.”

Khadir said, “(God saith), That ‘Allah’ of thine is My ‘Here am I,’ and that supplication and grief and ardour of thine is My messenger (to thee). Thy shifts and attempts to find a means (of gaining access to Me) were (in reality) My drawing (thee towards Me), and released thy feet (from the bonds of worldliness). Thy fear and love are the noose to catch My favour: beneath every ‘O Lord’ (of thine) is many a ‘Here am I’ (from Me).”

Far from this prayer is the soul of the fool, because to him it is not permitted to cry “O Lord.” On his mouth and heart are lock and bolt, to the end that he may not moan unto God in the hour of bale. He (God) gave to Pharaoh hundredfold possessions and riches, so that he claimed (Divine) might and majesty. In his whole life that man of evil nature felt no (spiritual) headache, lest he should moan unto God. God gave him all the empire of this world, (but) He did not give him grief and pain and sorrows. Grief is better than the empire of the world, so that you may call unto God in secret. The call of the griefless is from a frozen heart, the call of the grieving one is from rapture: (’Tis) to withdraw the voice under the lips, to bear in mind (one’s) origin and beginning; (’Tis) the voice become pure and sad, (crying) “O God!” and “O Thou whose help is besought!” and “O Helper!”[5]

Attributed to Imam ʿAlī bin Abītālib (d. 661)

Duʿā al-Mashlūl (The Supplication of the Ailing Person)

The earliest narration of this supplication is in Muhaj al-Daʿawāt wa Manhaj al-ʿIbādāt *by Sayyid ibn Ṭāwās (d. 1266). Sayyid ibn Ṭāwās provides a chain of narrators attributing the prayer to Imam ʿAlī bin Abītālib (d. 661). According to Majlesi al-Thānī (d. 1699), the story behind this prayer is this. A young person beats his father and steals his money. The heartbroken father goes on pilgrimage to Mecca, where he curses his son. Due to the father’s curse, the son contracts a serious disease. In his illness, the son spends many years begging his father for forgiveness. The father decides to go back to Mecca to pray for his son’s health. However, on his way to Mecca, the father dies; the son’s illness persists. Eventually, the son himself comes to Mecca, where he asks Imam ʿAlī for a supplication that will enable him to repent and heal. Imam ʿAlī teaches him* Duʿā al-Mashlūl.[6]

In the Name of God, the Compassionate, the Merciful:	Bismi Llāh al-Raḥmān al-Raḥim
My God! I beseech you by your name.	ʾAllāhuma ʾinnī ʾasʾaluka bismi-ka
In the Name of God, the Compassionate, the Merciful:	Bismi Llāh al-Raḥmān al-Raḥim
O Possessor of Glory and Honor,	Yā dhā'l-jalāli wa'l-ʾikrām
O Living One, O Self-Sustaining,	Yā Ḥayy, Yā Qayyūm
O Living One, there is no god but You.	Yā Ḥayy, yā lā ʾilāha ʾillā ʾanta
O He, of whom no one knows who he is,	Yā huwa, yā man lā yaʿlamu mā huwa
Nor how he is,	Wa lā kayfa huwa
Nor where He is,	Wa lā ʾayna huwa
And the One whose direction no one knows, but Him:	Wa lā ḥaythu huwa ʾillā huwa
O Possessor of this realm and the realm above,	Yā dhā'l-mulki wa' l-malakūt
O Possessor of Might and Dominion:	Yā dhā'l-ʿizzati wa' l-jabarūt
O King,[7]	Yā Malik
O Holy One,	Yā Quddūs
O Peace,	Yā Salām
O Faithful One,	Yā Muʾmin
O Protector,	Yā Muhaymin
O Almighty,	Yā ʿAzīz
O Compeller,	Yā Jabbār
O Supremely Great,	Yā Mutakabbir
O Creator,	Yā Ḵhāliq
O Maker,[8]	Yā Bāriʾ
O Shaper,	Yā Muṣawwir
O Provider of Goodness,	Yā Mufīd
O Manager [of everything],	Yā Mudabbir
O Severe One,	Yā Shadīd
O Originator,	Yā Mubdiʾ
O Restorer,	Yā Muʿīd
O One Who Begins [things],	Yā Mubīd

O Love,	Yā Wadūd
O Praised One,	Yā Maḥmūd
O Worshipped One,	Yā Ma'būd
O Distant One [O Transcendent One],	Yā Ba'īd
O Near One [O Immanent One],	Yā Qarīb
O Responder,	Yā Mujīb
O Protector,	Yā Raqīb
O Reckoner,	Yā Ḥasīb
O Innovator,	Yā Badī'
O Exalted,	Yā Rafī'
O Inaccessible,	Yā Manī'
O One Who Hears,	Yā Samī'
O Knowing,	Yā 'Alīm
O Forbearing,	Yā Ḥalīm
O Noble,	Yā Karīm
O Wise,	Yā Ḥakīm
O Eternal,	Yā Qadīm
O Excellent,	Yā 'Alī
O Exalted,	Yā 'Aẓīm
O Commiserating,	Yā Ḥannān
O Gracious,	Yā Mannān
O Condemner,	Yā Dayyān
O Recourse,	Yā Musta'ān
O Majestic,	Yā Jalīl
O Handsome,	Yā Jamīl
O Trustworthy,	Yā Wakīl
O Reliable,	Yā Kafīl
O Exemptor,	Yā Muqīl
O Deliverer,	Yā Munīl
O Noble,	Yā Nabīl
O Forerunner,	Yā Dalīl
O Guide,	Yā Hādī
O Apparent One,	Yā Bādī
O First,	Yā 'Awwal
O Last,	Yā 'Āḵir
O Visible,	Yā Ẓāhir
O Hidden,	Yā Bāṭin
O Steadfast,	Yā Qā'im
O Everlasting,	Yā Dā'im

O Knower,	Yā ʾĀlim
O Commander,	Yā Ḥākim
O Judge,	Yā Qāḍī
O Just One,	Yā ʿĀdil
O Separator,	Yā Fāṣil
O Connector,	Yā Wāṣil
O Immaculate,	Yā Ṭāhir
O Maker of Immaculateness,	Yā Muṭahhir
O Powerful,	Yā Qādir
O All-Powerful,	Yā Muqtadir
O Great,	Yā Kabīr
O Supremely Great,	Yā Mutakkabir
O One,	Yā Wāḥid
O Unique,	Yā ʾAḥad
O Everlasting,	Yā Ṣamad
O One who neither begat nor was begotten, and for whom there is no equal;	Yā man lam yalid wa lam yūlad wa lam yakun lahū kufuwan aḥad
And who neither takes a consort nor needs an assistant;	wa lam yakun lahū ṣāḥibatun wa lā kāna maʿahū wazīr
And who never needs to consult;	wa lā ittakhadha maʿahū mushīr
And who never relies on support.	wa lā iḥtāja ʾilā ẓahīr
And beside whom no other god stands:	wa lā kāna maʿahū min ʾilāh ghayruh
There is no god but You.	Lā ʾilāh illā ʾant a
You exceed whatever evildoers say about You.	Fa taʿālayt ʿammā yaqūl al-żālimūn ʿulwan kabīran
O Excellent,	Yā ʿAlī
O Lofty,	Yā Shāmikh
O Towering,	Yā Bāẕikh
O Opener,	Yā Fattāḥ
O Breather,	Yā Naffāḥ
O Tranquil,	Yā Murtāḥ
O Bestower of opportunities,	Yā Mufarrij
O Helper,	Yā Nāṣir
O Victor,	Yā Muntaṣir
O Perceptive One,	Yā Mudrik
O Death-dealer,	Yā Muhlik
O Avenger,	Yā Muntaqim
O Initiator,	Yā Bāʿith
O Inheritor,	Yā Wārith

O Seeker,	Yā Ṭālib
O Vanquisher,	Yā Ghālib
O One from whom no one can escape,	Yā man lā yafūtuhu hārib
O All-Relenting,	Yā Tāwwāb
O All-Accepting,	Yā ʾAwwāb
O Freely Giving,	Yā Wāhhāb
O Cause of all causes,	Yā Musabbibʿl-ʾasbāb
O Opener of all doors,	Yā Mufattiḥaʿl-ʾabwāb
O One who answers however called,	Yā man ḥaysumā duʿīya ʾajāb
O Purity,	Yā Ṭahūr
O Gratitude,	Yā Shakūr
O Forgiveness,	Yā ʿAfuw
O Absolution,	Yā Ghafūr
O Light of Lights,	Yā Nūr al-Nūr
O Contemplator of all affairs,	Yā Mudabbr al-ʾumūr
O Gracious,	Yā Laṭīf
O Aware,	Yā Khabīr
O Responder,	Yā Mujīr
O Giver of Light,	Yā Munīr
O All-Seeing,	Yā Baṣīr
O Supporting,	Yā Dhahīr
O Great One,	Yā Kabīr
O Alone,	Yā Witr
O Singularity,	Yā Fard
O Eternal,	Yā ʾAbad
O Foundation,	Yā Sanad
O Only,	Yā Ṣamad
O Sufficient,	Yā Kāfī
O Healer,	Yā Shāfī
O Loyal,	Yā Wāfī
O Liberator,	Ya Muʿāfī
O Doer of the Beautiful,	Yā Muḥsin
O Beautifier,	Yā Mujmil
O All-Benevolent,	Yā Munʿim
O Bestower of Bounty,	Yā Mufaḍil
O All-noble,	Yā Mutakarrim
O All-Singular,	Yā Mutafarrid
O One who Excels and Overcomes,	Yā man ʿalā fa-qahar

O One Who Owns and Apportions all things,	Yā man malaka fa-qadar
O Concealer and Revealer,	Yā man baṭana fa-khabar
O Rewarder of worshippers,	Yā man ʿubida fa-shakar
O Absolver of transgressors,	Yā man ʿuṣiya fa-qafar
O One whom thought fails to contain, whom eyes cannot see, and whom nothing escapes,	Yā man lā taḥwih [yaḥwih] al-fikar wa lā yudrikuhū baṣar wa lā yakhfā ʿalayh ʾathar
O Provider for all humans,	Yā rāziq al-bashar
O Measurer of all fates,	Yā muqaddir kulli qadar
O Lofty in Esteem,	Yā ʿālī al-makān
O Firm in Foundation,	Yā shadīd al-ʾarkān
O Changer of the Times,	Yā mubaddil al-zamān
O Accepter of Sacrifice,	Yā qābil al-qurbān
O Possessor of Benevolence and Virtue,	Yā dhā'l-manni wa'l-iḥsān
O Possessor of Might and Domination,	Yā dhā'l-ʿizzati wa'l-sulṭān
O Compassionate, O Merciful,	Yā Raḥim, Yā Raḥmān
O One who Commands All Days,	Yā man huwa kulla yawmin fī shaʿnin
O Who is not distracted from one thing by another,	Yā man lā yashghaluhū shaʿnun an shaʿnin
O Highest in Rank,	Yā ʿaẓīm al-shaʿn
O Omnipresent,	Yā man huwa bi-kulli makān
O Omni-hearing,	Yā samiʿa al-āṣwāt
O Responder to all pleas,	Yā mujība al-daʿawāt
O Granter of all that is sought,	Yā munjiḥa al-ṭalibāt
O Provider of all needs,	Yā qāḍiya al-ḥājāt
O Sender of all blessings,	Yā munzil al-barakāt
O Who has compassion for tears,	Yā rāḥima al-ʿabarāt
O Who is easy on the falling,	Yā muqīl al-ʿasarāt
O Remover of sorrow,	Yā kāshif al-kurubāt
O Owner of all that is good,	Yā walī al-hasanāt
O Who elevates ranks,	Yā rāfiʾ al-darajāt
O Giver of all queries,	Yā muʾtī al-suʾlāt
O Enlivener of the dead,	Yā muḥyī al-amwāt
O Gatherer of scattered things,	Yā jāmiʾa al-shatāt
O Discerner of all intentions,	Yā muṭṭaliʾan ʿala al-nīyyāt
O Restorer of whatever is lost,	Yā rādda mā qad fāt

O One in the presence of whom sounds are never confused,	Yā man lā tashtabihu ʿalayhiʾ aṣwāt
O One Who Inquiries do not bewilder and darkness never occludes,	Yā man lā tuzjiruhu al-masʾalāt, wa lā taghshāhu al-ẓulumāt
O Light of the earth and the heavens,	Yā nūra al-arḍ wa al-samāwāt
O Giver of abundant blessings,	Yā sābigha al-niʿam
O Remover of desolation,	Yā dāfiʿa al-niqam
O Initiator of all life,	Yā bariʾ al-nasam
O Gatherer of all nations,	Yā jāmiʿ al-umam
O Curer of all ailments,	Yā shāfiya al-saqam
O Creator of light and darkness,	Yā khāliqa al-nūr wa'l-zulam
O Munificent and Generous,	Yā ahl al-jud wa al-karam
O He whose Throne no foot reaches,	Yā man lā yaṭaʾu ʿarshahā qadam
O Most Generous of all Generous,	Yā ajwad'l-ajwadīn
O Most Noble of the Noble,	Yā akram'l-akramīn
O Best Hearing of the listeners,	Yā asma' al-shāmiʿīn
O You Seeing of all viewers,	Yā abṣar'l-nāẓirīn
O rescuer of those who call You,	Yā jāra'l-mustajīrīn
O granter of safety to those in fear,	Yā amān'l-khāʾifīn
O supporter of those who take refuge,	Yā ẓahra'l-lājīn
O Friend of the faithful,	Yā walī al-muʿminīn
O rescuer of the helpless,	Yā ghiāth al-mustaghīthīn
O Ultimate goal of the seekers,	Yā ghāyata'l-ṭālibīn
O Companion to the strangers,	Yā ṣāḥib kulli gharīb
O keeper of company with the lonely,	Yā munis kulli waḥīd
O Refuge of the banished,	Yā maljaʾ kulli ṭarīd
O Shelter of the homeless,	Yā maʾwā kulli sharīd
O Custodian to the lost,	Yā ḥāfiẓa kulli ḍāll
O One filled with compassion for the elderly,	Yā rāḥim al-shaykh al-kabīr
O nourisher of the infants,	Yā rāziq'l-ṭifl al-ṣaghīr
O healer of broken bones,	Yā jābir'l-ʿaẓim al-kasīr
O liberator of all captured,	Yā fākka kulli asīr
O enricher of every pauper,	Yā mughniya al-bāʾis al-faqīr

O protector of every fearful caller from despair,	Yā ʿiṣmata al-khāʾif al-mustajīr
O He who governs and determines,	Yā mān lahū al-tadbīr wa'l-taqdīr
O He for Whom the difficult is easy,	Yā man al-ʿasīr ʿalayhi sahlun yasir
O He who is never in need of explanation,	Yā man lā yaḥtāju ilā tafsīr
O He who over all things has power,	Yā man huwa ʿalā kulli shayʾin qadīr
O He who of all things has knowledge,	Yā man huwa bikulli shayʾin khabīr
O He who can see all things,	Yā man huwa bi-kulli shayʾin baṣīr
O Dispatcher of the winds,	Yā mursil al-riyāḥ
O Unraveler of every dawning day,	Yā fāliq al-īṣbāḥ
O Resurrector of the souls,	Yā bāʿth al-āʾrwāḥ
O Exemplar of Generosity and Contentment,	Yā dhā'l-jūd wa'l-samāḥ
O He whose hand holds all keys,	Yā man biyadihī kullu miftāḥin
O Hearer of all sounds,	Yā sāmiʿa kulli ṣawtin
O Restorer of all losses,	Yā sābiqa kulli fawtin
O Enlivener of every person after death,	Yā muḥyiya kulli nafsin baʿda almawti
O Upon Whom I rely in my hardship,	Yā ʿuddatī fī shiddtī
O Guardian among strangers,	Yā ḥāfiẓī fī ghurbat
O Companion in solitude,	Yā muʾnisī fī waḥdatī
O Sponsor of Blessings,	Yā waliyyī fī niʾmatī
O Haven from disparate paths, when close ones leave me, and when all others let me down,	Yā kahfī ḥīna tuʿyīnī almadhāhibu, wa tusallimunī al-aqāribu, wa yakhdhulunī kullu ṣāḥibin
O Upholder of those who have no one uphold them,	Yā ʿimāda man lā ʿimāda lahū
O Support of those who have no support,	Yā sanada man lā sanada lahū
O Store for those who have no store,	Yā dhukhra man lā dhukhra lahū
O Sanctuary for those who have no sanctuary,	Yā ḥirza man lā ḥirza lahū
O Cave for those who have no cave,	Yā kahf man lā kahf lahū
O Treasure for those who have no treasure,	Yā kanz min lā kanz lahū

O Upholder of whoever has no upholder,	Yā rukna man lā rukna lahū
O Answerer of the cries of those who have no one to answer their cries,	Yā ghiyātha man la ghiyātha lahū
O Backer of those who have no backer,	Yā jārr min lā jārr lahū
O My close neighbor,	Yā Jārīa'l-laṣīq
O My strong foundation,	Yā Rukni'l-wathīq
O My God in truth,	Yā Ilāhi bi'l-taḥqīq
O Lord of the Ancient House,	Yā Rabbi'l-bayti'l-ʿantīq
O Kind One,	Yā Shafīq
O Friend . . .	Yā Rafīq

[The thirty-some verses omitted here are a rehearsal of God's mighty acts by means of prophets.]

O God! O God! O God!	Yā Allāh, Yā Allāh, Yā Allāh,
O Compassionate! O Compassionate! O Compassionate!	Yā Raḥmān, Yā Raḥmān, Yā Raḥmān
O Merciful! O Merciful! O Merciful!	Yā Raḥīm, Yā Raḥīm, Yā Raḥīm
O Possessor of Majesty and Generosity! O Possessor of Majesty and Generosity! O Possessor of Majesty and Generosity!	Yā dhā'l-jalāl wa'l-ikrām! Yā dhā'l-jalāl wa'l-ikrām! Yā dhā'l-jalāl wa'l-ikrām!
By Him, by Him, by Him, by Him, by Him, by Him!	Bi-hī, bi-hī, bi-hī, bi-hī, bi-hī, bi-hī,
I beseech You by every name that You have named Yourself or You have sent down in any of Your Books, or that You left a trace of in the knowledge of the unseen which You possess; by the Might of Your Throne to the Utmost Compassion in Your Book; by that which if every tree on the earth were to become writing pens and the oceans were multiplied sevenfold, Your words would never be exhausted.	Asāluka bikulli ismin sammayta bihī nafsaka aw anzaltahū fī shayʾin min kutubika aw istaʾtharta bihī fī ʿilmi'l-ghaybi ʿindaka wa bimaʿāqidi'l-ʿizzi min arshika wa bimuntahā'l-raḥmati min kitābika wa bimā law anna mā fī'l-arḍi min shajaratin aqlāmun wa'l-baḥru yamudduhū min baʿdihī sabʿatu abḥurin mā nafidat kalimātu allāhi.

Indeed, God is Mighty, Wise.	Inna Allāha ʿazīzun ḥakīm
And I beseech You by Your beautiful names, which You have mentioned in Your Book.	Wa asāluka bi-asmāʾikaʾl-ḥusnā alatī naʿattahā fī kitābika
And You said, "God has beautiful names, call Him with those."	Fa qulta: wa li-Llāhiʾl-asmāʾ l- ḥusnā fā dʿūhu bihā
And You said, "Call me, and I answer you."	Wa qulta udʿūnī astajib lakum
And You said, "When my servants ask, I am near, answering the callers as they call on Me."	wa qulta wa idhā saʾalaka ʿibādī ʿannī faʾinnī qarīb ujību daʿwataʾl-dāʿī idhā daʿā.
And you said, "O my servants who have wronged yourselves, never despair of God's Mercy. Indeed, God forgives all sins. Indeed, He is Forgiving and Compassionate."	Wa qulta qul yā ʿībīdīya alladhīna aṣrafū ʿalā anfusihim lā taqnatū min rahmati allāhi. Inna Allāha yaghfiru al-dhūnūba jamīʾan. Innahū huwa'l-ghafūr al-rahīm
And I beseech You, my God!	Wa ana asʾaluka yā llahī
And I call You, my Lord!	Wa adʾuka yā rabbi
And I have hope in You, my Master!	Wa arjūka yā sayyidī
And I expect that my supplication will be granted, my Lord, as You promised me.	Wa aṭmaʾu fi ijābatī yā mawlāya kamā waʿadtanī
And I call You, as You commended me to.	Wa qad daʿawtuka kamā amartanī
Do unto me what You should, O Noble Lord.	Fafʿal bi mā anta ahluhū yā karim
All praise belongs to God, Lord of the worlds.	Wa al-hamdu lillahi rabbi al-alamīn
And blessings upon Muhammad and all his family.	Wa ṣalli allāhu ʿalā Muḥammad wa ālihī ajmaʿīn.

Attributed to the Prophet Muhammad

Jawshan al-Kabīr (The Greater Armor)

Not studied during the 2021 seminar, yet a fine example of Muslim devotional literature relevant to the theme of "naming God," is the one-hundred-stanza supplication Jawshān al-kabīr

(The Greater Armor)—a hadith of the Prophet transmitted through ʿAlī.[9] *Its title implies that it is to be recited as preparation for physical or spiritual struggle.*

In structure, the Jawshān al-Kabīr *consists of one hundred stanzas, each made up of ten invocations in parallel format, each concluding with "Praise be to You! There is no god but you! Ultimate refuge: save us from the Fire!" (or a variant of this).*[10] *The stanzas are grouped in quartets; each stanza-quartet is inaugurated by the invocation, "O God! I beseech You by means of Your Names." By virtue of these two regularly recurring refrains, a unique rhythm is established for the litany as a whole. In every quartet, the first stanza consists of "single names"; in the subsequent three stanzas, the names consist of two or more words and thus are increasingly more complex.*

Each set of ten invocations is unified by the length of the honorifics it features, plus the word order, word endings, and other techniques by which they have been created. Thus, a particular rhythm and rhyme is created for each stanza; sound patterns and grammatical devices, rather than any traditional list, determine the order of the Beautiful Names in this supplication. Presented here, by way of example, are the Jawshan's *first five stanzas.*[11]

	Bismillāhi ar-Rahmān ar-Rahīm	In the Name of God: the Compassionate, the Merciful:
1	Allahumi innī asʾaluka bi asmāʾika	O God! I beseech You by means of Your Names:
	Yā Allāh	O God
	Yā Rahmān	O Compassionate
	Yā Rahīm	O Merciful
	Yā ʿAlīm	O Knowing
	Yā Halīm	O Gentle
	Yā ʿAẓīm	O Splendid
	Yā Hakīm	O Wise
	Yā Qadīm	O Infinite
	Yā Muqīm	O Persistent
	Yā Karīm	O Noble
	Subhānaka yā lā ilāha illā anta'l-amānu'l-amānu khallisnā min an-nār.	Praise be to You! There is no god but you! Ultimate Refuge:[12] save us from the Fire!
2	Yā Sayyid as-sādāt	O Lord of lords!
	Yā Mujīb ad-daʾawāt	O Answerer of supplication;
	Yā Walīya'l-Hasanāt	O Preserver of good deeds;
	Yā Rafīʾaʾd-darajāt	O Loftiest in degree;
	Yā ʿĀzīm al-barakāt	O Bestower of blessings;
	Yā Ghāfirāʾl-hatīʾāt	O Forgiver of sins;

	Yā Dāfi᾽a'l-baliyyāt	O Repeller of afflictions;
	Yā Sāmi᾽ā'l-aswāt	O Hearer of sounds;
	Yā Mu᾽tiyā'l-mas᾽ūlāt	O Granter of requests;
	Yā ʿĀlimā᾽sirri wa'l hafiyyāt	O Knower of secrets and mysteries—
	Subhānaka yā lā ilāha illā anta'l-amānu'l-amānu khallisnā min an-nār.	Praise be to You! There is no god but you! Ultimate Refuge: save us from the Fire!
3	Yā Khayr al-ghāfirīn	O Best of Pardoners;
	Yā Khayr an-nāsirīn	O Best of Helpers;
	Yā Khayr al-hākimīn	O Best of Judges;
	Yā Khayr al-fātihīn	O Best of Openers;
	Yā Khayr adh-dhākirīn	O Best Rememberer;
	Yā Khayr al-wārithīn	O Best of Inheritors;
	Yā Khayr al-hāmidīn	O Best of Praisers;
	Yā Khayr al-rāziqīn	O Best of Providers;
	Yā Khayr al-fasilīn	O Best of Decision-makers;[13]
	Yā Khayr al-muhsinīn	O Best of the Doers of the Beautiful—
	Subhānaka yā lā ilāha illā anta'l-amānu'l-amānu khallisnā min an-nār.	Praise be to You! There is no god but you! Ultimate Refuge: save us from the Fire!
4	Yā man lahu'l-izzu wa'l-jamāl	O One of Might and Beauty;
	Yā man lahu'l-mulku wa'l-jalāl	O Possessor of Dominion and Glory;
	Yā man lahu'l-qudratu wa᾽l-kamāl	O Owner of Power and Perfection;
	Yā man huwa'l-kabīru'l-muta᾽āl	O He who is Sublime, Most High;
	Yā man huwa'l-shadīdu'l-mihāl	O He whose stratagems are most powerful;
	Yā man huwa'l-shadīdu'l-᾽iqāb	O He whose chastisement is most severe;
	Yā man huwa sharī᾽u'l-hisāb	O He who calls to account most swiftly;
	Yā man huwa ʿindahū husnu'l-thuwāb	O He with whom is the best of rewards;
	Yā man huwa ʿindahū ummu'l-kitāb	O He with whom is the Mother of the Book;

Yā man huwa yunshi᾽u's-sahāba'l-thiqāl	O He who raises aloft the heavy clouds—
Subhānaka yā lā ilāha illā anta'l-amānu'l-amānu khallisnā min an-nār.	Praise be to You, than whom there is no god! Ultimate Refuge: save us from the Fire!
5 Wa as᾽aluka bi asmā᾽ika	And I beseech You by means of Your Names:
Yā Hannān	O Tender One
Yā Mannān	O Benefactor
Yā Dayyān	O Judge
Yā Ghufrān	O Much-Forgiving One
Yā Burhān	O Proof
Yā Sultān	O Ruler
Yā Subhān	O Glorious
Yā Musta᾽ān	O One Implored for Help
Yā Dhā'l-manni wa'l-bayān	O Bounteous Offerer of Clear Evidence
Yā Dhā'l-amān	O Giver of quarter—
Subhānaka yā lā ilāha illā anta'l-amānu'l-amānu khallisnā min an-nār.	Praise be to You! There is no god but you! Ultimate Refuge: save us from the Fire!

Notes

1. Victor Danner, trans., *Ibn ʿAṭā᾽illāh's Sufi Aphorisms* (Leiden: E. J. Brill, 1973), 32.

2. Ibn ʿAṭā᾽illāh al-Iskandarī, *The Key to Salvation: A Sufi Manual of Invocation,* trans. Mary Ann Khoury Danner (Cambridge: Islamic Texts Society, 1996; reprint 2012), 45.

3. al-Iskandarī, 51.

4. al-Iskandarī, 79–87.

5. Reynold A. Nicholson, trans., *The Mathnawi of Jalaluddin Rumi,* book 3 (London: Luzac, 1930), lines 189–206.

6. This translation and transliteration of *Duʿā al-Mashlūl* is the result of the editor's collaboration with Professor Hossein Kamaly, PhD (Hartford International University for Religion and Peace) and Imam Rasoul Naghavi Nia, PhD (Mufid Academic Seminary), with reference to dua.org. Responsibility for any remaining errors lies with the editor.

7. In the Qur᾽an, see Sūrat'l-Ḥashr (59):23 for this name and the eight names following it.

8. Please note the change in tone.

9. The chain of transmission has been traced (albeit somewhat weakly) through Zayn al-ʿĀbidīn (Alī ibn al-Ḥusayn: a grandson of the Prophet) and his father Ḥusayn to Alī. For a scholarly analysis of the *Jawshān al-kabīr*, see Ahmet Eren Kademoğlu, *The Textual and the*

Spiritual Structure of the Jawshān al-Kabīr: A Study on Jawshān al-Kabīr and Its Translation (Licence diss., Rome: Pontifico Instituto di Studi Arabi e d'Islamistica, 2000).

10. For a complete translation, see Şükran Vahide, trans., *A Supplication of the Prophet Muhammad (Peace and blessings be upon him) al-Jawshan al-Kabîr* (Istanbul: Sözler, 2003). "Ultimate refuge" aptly conveys the meaning of the construct *amānu'l-amānu* but provides no clue to the English reader as to what is going on in the text rhetorically. The same can be said of other translations of this refrain—for example, "Mercy, mercy . . ." (Vahide) and "In you lies security and peace" (Kademoğlu). The very literal "Security of the security" conveys the construct's sound-vision but is otherwise awkward.

11. The preceding explanation and the translation of the portion of the *Jawshān al-Kabīr* provided here as an example are informed by Lucinda Mosher, "Supplication as Agent and Fruit of Transfomation for Bediüzzaman Said Nursī," in *The Companion to Said Nursi Studies*, eds. Ian S. Markham and Zeyneb Sayilgan (Eugene, OR: Pickwick, 2017), 146–60.

12. See note 10.

13. That is, in matters of justice. From the root verb *to sever, to segregate.*

Part Four

Reflection

13

Conversations in Cyberspace

A Sampler from the Virtual Circle

Lucinda Mosher

"To nobody's surprise, because we've all been to the Building Bridges Seminar previously, we spent a lot of time posing theological questions to the other," one participant asserted. "When it came to God's Names, we dealt with matters of translation and meaning, and the relation of one Name to another," one participant noted. "We had less time together than would normally have been the case," another observed. "That was frustrating. Yet our time together was also very rich. So much about the seminar is about the building of friendships. It is a really special conversation that has stretched out over nearly twenty years!"

The Building Bridges Seminar has long been described as an exercise in development of a "virtuous circle"—in this case, an exercise in "listening to each other listening to God" through which participants "become better able to listen to each other." In 2021 the challenge was to be a circle that was both virtuous and virtual! Invitations were limited to scholars who had participated in one or more of the previous convenings. Those who had accepted were situated around the globe and would be joining the online discussion from Australia, Belgium, Bosnia and Herzegovina, Colombia, France, Germany, Ghana, Kenya, Qatar, Switzerland, the United Kingdom, the United States, and more. All met together online via Zoom for three and a half hours on day 1 to hear and discuss a series of formal presentations. Dialogical close reading of texts ensued on days 2, 3, and 4—participants having been assigned to one of three predetermined small groups, each with its own daily, two-and-a-half-hour Zoom call. This meant—as moderator Dan Madigan put it when opening the summary plenary on Friday (another two-and-a-half-hour Zoom session)—that for most of the week, participants "had been in their separate universes." Friday's plenary provided an opportunity to hear how things had gone. Six reporters (a Muslim and a Christian from each group) took unique approaches to digesting what had emerged during many hours of dialogical close reading of verses from the Bible and the Qur'an, excerpts from Christian and Muslim theological writings, and examples of devotional literature.

This chapter offers the reader an opportunity to overhear Building Bridges Seminar conversations about naming God. It draws heavily upon the six summary reports, supplementing them with excerpts from the opening plenary discussions and the midweek small-group study sessions. As one reporter noted, each day of small-group work may have focused on a particular sort of material (scriptural, theological, devotional), but conversations were free-ranging. That will be apparent in what follows. This cyberspace sampler is organized according to the three categories of literature engaged through dialogical close reading, but also, according to topics around which engagement was lively and insightful. As is the custom of the Building Bridges Seminar, the Chatham House Rule obtains: participants are quoted or paraphrased without attribution.

Close Reading of Scripture on Naming God

"God" versus "God's Names"

"I am fascinated by the use of the verb *to be* in Exodus 3:14," said a Muslim scholar. "God *is*; God *will be*. God's Name is a promise! God's Name is not just a label. It is a dialogical narrative in history."

What is the relation between God and God's Names? What *are* the relations between God and God's Names in eternity? In various ways, each group wrestled with such questions. One scholar noted that both traditions draw on a range of theories of naming. There is agreement, she stressed, that "the identity between God and God's Names is radically different from the relationship of any 'thing' to its names." There also are clear differences between the traditions. For example, she explained:

> In the Christian depiction of the revelation of God, at least some of God's Names are not just given by God to God. They are used of God by God and are used to address God by God. This is the eternal conversation of the Trinity. In Christian scripture, we see some of the Names of God—including Father, Son, and Spirit (but not only those)—are used to talk about God and to tell us *who God is* (in the classic view of revelation). The Names are also used *by* God to talk *to* God. The Names allow us to eavesdrop, as it were, upon the divine conversation and to offer a divine

conversation as the pattern or the place within which prayer and worship might be able to take place.

Hagar's Naming of God

During the week, noted a Muslim reporter, two paradoxes had arisen. The first paradox "is that 'naming' takes place *in* time, with actions *in* time. But God is *beyond* time." The second paradox is that "naming" is both local/relational and universal/abstract. "We pondered the question of how something very particular becomes universal," he explained. For one of the Christians, the question of the local versus the universal is thought-provoking, in that, in the book of Genesis, Hagar's personal, local experience of being seen by God turns into a more universal statement about God in Exodus.

In fact, the Genesis account of Hagar and her experience of God—and the many questions this narrative provoked—was galvanizing, said one group's Christian reporter. Especially intriguing had been the conversation between Hagar and the angel: Hagar's way of naming God, she said, "caught our attention because it came out of her affliction. It was interesting to us that, in this passage, the Divine is named 'God Who Sees.' More often, it is 'God-Who-Hears.'" The Christian texts brought out the tradition of God as creator, she noted. "God is the One who reveals self through creation."

Indeed, in Genesis, Hagar appears to devise a name for God, with the scriptural text apparently expressing no disapproval of her doing so. This was surprising to some of the Muslims in the circle. They suggested, in Islamic tradition, there is a tendency to think that human beings should limit themselves to calling on God only using the Names by which God has named Godself. Some of the Christians responded that the Christian tradition appears, on the whole, to be less cautious than the Islamic tradition in this matter.

In effect, one participant observed, the passage from Rumi's *Mathnawi*—the point of which is that our calling upon God is actually a response *from* God—was an apt counterbalance for the Christian scriptural text about Hagar. (He called the two items "bookends.") "Hagar realized that her calling out to God had been seen. When we realize that God has seen us, we have (ipso facto) seen God!"

Relationality

A Christian noted that the notion of *takhalluq bi-akhlāq Allāh* (being molded by the [moral] qualities of God) had featured in his group's discussions several times, as well as *ta'alluh* (conforming to God). "These are tantalizing notions," he remarked as he asked Muslims in the circle to offer further clarification. One replied that the notion that God relates to humanity through humanity's relationship to God is, in a sense, *ta'alluh*. He then referred to a hadith the seminar had studied, explaining:

> In it, the Prophet says to Aisha, "There is this one name of God." She says, "Tell it to me." He says, "It's not for you!" She asks multiple times. She calls upon God. The Prophet says she used "that name" but doesn't tell her which it is! What does it mean? It is such a grave matter, yet he is so playful! What does it mean? Maybe the highest name is not a "name" but a condition of relationality. And when you call upon God in that way, you've got the Name.

Another Muslim celebrated Aisha's determination to call upon God even if she doesn't know the right name:

> I like her confidence in saying to God, "I call upon you by all of the Names I know—and by all of the Names I don't know!" She's getting around the limitation. She's determined that God will hear her. She has a confidence that, even if she doesn't know the right name, and even if that name is not for her, as a human being with her own love and desire for God, God will hear her! In the same way that Hagar becomes confident that God has heard her, has seen her, she has been seen. She is not forgotten!

Relationship is specified through narrative elements, one of the Christian scholars declared, pointing to the biblical story of Moses as evidence. He noted how frequently the seminar had teetered between affirmation and denial of the "efficacious relationality" between personal experience and affirmation of God's identity. "This sort of back and forth is right there in the Exodus narrative we studied," he reminded the group. "In Exodus 33, God tells Moses: 'you cannot see my face and live.' Interestingly, this is seven verses after we read that Moses spoke face-to-face with God! And Moses goes on to see God again!" Fundamental to both traditions, he sensed, is "movement between denying that we can see God, that we can know God, that we can understand God; then affirming that we can, of course—because God wants that; and nothing is impossible with God."

In the Exodus narrative, God tells Moses to take off his sandals because he is on holy ground; Moses is told not to come any closer; and then God's

Name is revealed. These elements, a Christian explained, establish that the human/Divine relationship is not a symmetrical one:

> It is fully reciprocal. It is a kind of asymmetry in which God's initiative is always prior. Our naming of God seems to depend on acknowledging this asymmetry. The Aisha hadith makes that very clear; because she wants to know (out of theological curiosity—which is the best kind of curiosity), "Could I please know the best name of God?" The Prophet says, "No! That's not for you! That's not for theological curiosity!" She tells him that she has done the ablutions and two cycles of prayer, so she gets into the right relation to God. It is the right attitude in which she approaches calling on God's Names. And then she does so in the fullest possible sense in which one could do it. But I think the point is not that she mentions all of the Names; therefore, she must have mentioned the right one. Rather, the point is that she does so with the right attitude—an attitude that acknowledges this asymmetry. And that seems to be the point of all the "naming" stories in our traditions.

Another Muslim concurred, noting that the asymmetry between God and humanity is absolute. "We are God's creatures. Therefore, God's omnipotence and our knowledge can never be measured on the same scale—a point made at all times by the Divine Names. Our dignity resides with the fact that we are the free gifts of God—and not on the same scale, but just the gratuitous creatures of God's promise and love."

Close Reading of Theological Writings on Naming God

God's Names "are privileged theological spaces where our relationship to God can be thought and lived," a Muslim asserted. They are reminders that human relationship to God is absolutely asymmetrical: God can give totally; humanity cannot. "God is the ultimate Giver," he explained. The Divine relationship within the world is continuous and uninterrupted. "God is continually in us and for us. God is continually active in the world."

In fact, one group approached the Names of God as a gift, specifically: "God's generous kenosis of self-limiting, which is nevertheless a pattern of self-sharing. Such self-limiting is not a closing-down; it is an outpouring, a sending out, a spreading." A gift has a purpose, this reporter continued. "To understand the gift, we need to think about what it is for and how it can draw us closer to God. This does not mean we are restricted to a functional approach to understanding of God's Names. It does not close down ontologically prior questions of God's Divine Names, as it were, apart from creation. But in fact it opens up onto them."

Call and Response

One group gave considerable attention to the complex dynamics of call and response. To understand what human beings are doing when they call upon God's Name requires understanding of "what God is doing, before and within and underneath," noted one of the Christians—particularly "the radical priority of the divine initiative." For example, she explained, Augustine describes the Holy Spirit "as the wind which fills our sail in our journey to God." However, "we still need to tilt that sail to catch that wind—to do some work, patiently perhaps, putting in the oars. It is God who works first; and always God is working; but we have to work with that."

In Islam, explained a Muslim scholar, we find the notion of the "Highest" or "Greatest" Name of God—about which many interpretations are offered. He clarified:

> Some say that what it is will depend on your emotional or physical status. The highest Name of God (for you) relates to your status, your condition. In the biblical account, Hagar was in a situation where she wanted to have that confidence that God Almighty is going to help her. What we learn in Rumi's *Mathnawi* is that both grief and happiness—in fact, all conditions and phases of life—are related to Names of Almighty God.

On Sharing in God's Names

What does it mean to be getting to know the Names of God? What is involved on the human side? A Christian scholar thoroughly enjoyed the answer provided by al-Ghazālī in *The Ninety-Nine Beautiful Names of God*, wherein the point seemed to be that getting to know the Name of God is only possible through sharing: "So it is a form of participatory knowledge, which develops in stages." In the first stage knowledge of God comes only by hearsay—through what others share with us by means of witness and instruction. In the second stage knowledge of God becomes an intellectual certainty. However, this is insufficient "because this presence of God through sharing transforms our heart in such a way that it awakens a desire for God. And a desire for God to be illuminated already includes the reality of God. It is a desire that is triggered by the lack of God's reality. It is a desire that already participates in the reality of God." In the third stage human beings become companions of the heavenly host of angels, thus sharing proximity to God. Hence, this observer concluded, "the naming of God is woven into the texture of a structured process of getting to know God. Intellectual knowing of God is but the first stage. Getting to know God must go through our affections. That seems to be the most important form of transformation."

From a Reformation-theological point of view, a Christian explained, "in Christ, God speaks as pure promise, as pure Gospel. And what is the content of that Gospel? Godself—in relation to those to whom God promises. Therefore, there is a form of continuity. It has a narratival shape; it is the dynamics of history that are held together by the narrative of God's promise."

God's Names as Boundaries for the Visible

"The Divine Names define states of spiritual life," a Muslim explained as he took note of a hierarchical relation between the God's Names, a sense in which they are boundaries for the visible. "This hierarchy reflects an intimacy with the creator that is present in the use of the Divine Names in rituals of the faithful. That kind of hierarchy emerges in considering the possibility of knowing God's essence." In al-Ghazālī, he observed, "we read of the possibility of knowing the essence of God through the heart." Thomas Aquinas says something similar: "however, this knowing can only be partial now; it can only be complete in the hereafter."

In reflecting upon the relation of the Divine Names to human comportment, a Christian scholar asserted that the point is not to imitate God but rather to conform to God. His Muslim colleague asked for clarification of the difference between imitation and conformity and the reason for emphasizing it.

The Christian replied, saying that "medieval theologian Thomas à Kempis suggested that Christians could emulate the life of Christ in terms of the works of mercy, in terms of healing, in terms of looking after the poor, and so on." Reformation theology said, to the contrary, that none of this could be done unless enabled by God's grace. To be conformed to Christ is to experience a radical change through which one's human heart becomes consonant with the Divine love—and then, also, with the other Divine attributes. "It is something that God must give. This action must come from God. We respond to it. Continued practice will make us able to do these things; but our heart has to be changed. It's a question of the formation of a person. A good person will do good works; good works will never make a good person."

To the Muslim scholar, this sounded very much like al-Ghazālī's notion of "shares" in the meanings of God's Names. "It strikes me as al-Ghazālī's first share, in which you have to rid your heart of worldly detachments. You have to repel vice in order to make room for virtue. You don't actively acquire the virtue; you actively work on eliminating the vice. You work on renouncing the world in your heart, so that your heart will then, by God's grace, become attached to God."

"I see that as his second share," countered the Christian scholar. "Ghazālī's first share, I think, is a rational proof; it is *alam* in a proper argument. The second share? That's the transformation of the heart. Rational doubts are taken away; but now comes the bigger thing: is your heart also transformed?"

"Well," the Muslim explained,

> typically, al-Ghazālī speaks of "demonstrative unveiling." That's the ineluctable certitude one gets from philosophical, rational thinking. "Unveiling" is the certainty of the heart that one experiences through direct witnessing or disclosure. Typically, al-Ghazālī combines the philosophical and the mystical. He says that to truly know your powerlessness, you actually begin to grasp Divine omnipotence. The first share is to *know* that one is a servant characterized by a particular deficiency or imperfection. It's a recognition of vice or weakness. The second share is true attraction to the divine side. So the first is not a rational-demonstrative sort of engagement with God's Names, technically speaking. It's a bit of a combined, hybrid form of knowledge. So, to use your term: "I conform to God when I know that I am powerless; I do not conform to God when I affirm my power as an independent reality. Once I know I'm powerless, then through my servanthood I can communicate God's love." This is a core concept in the Islamic tradition, too: God loves to be known; so God creates the world and is to be known as the driving force behind creation.

From a Reformation-theological perspective, the Christian responded,

> the law demonstrates to you that you can't fulfill the law. However, it also says that you are totally dependent on God's grace in being enabled to fulfill the law. Now you do so not because it's commanded. Rather, you do so out of *desire* and love. I think that is very close to al-Ghazālī's second share, in which you have this longing to possess these attributes. It is inconceivable that a heart be filled with high regard for (and being illuminated by) such an attribute without a longing for this attribute following upon it. That kind of "being filled" is the fulfillment of my desire—not my achieving of it—and is at the root of all thankfulness to God for whatever I am and what I do.

His Muslim colleague seemed to concur.

God's Names, Power, and Gender

The beauty of God's Names was a recurring theme. Beauty may be defined as the good that claims us by its attractiveness. Hence, God's beautiful Names are powerful. Likewise, one group noted, the power of beautiful devotion—music included—is emotional and visceral. They saw this in the relation of God's voice and Names in expressions of lament and complaint. Excerpts from Rumi's *Mathnawi* and the biblical books of Jeremiah and Isaiah had provided important evidence of ways in which God's Name is present in and to the experience of grief.

One of the women noted the heavily masculine nature of the language for God in certain texts under study. "Some Christians say that the overemphasis on maleness can be idolatrous," she said. Indeed, said another participant, "the Names of God are names of power—of strength, of lordliness, of domination. That opens the possibility of serious misuse." Exploiting these Names of God for human rather than Divine purposes; the question of gender, particularly in the naming of God; masculinity and the question of power: these are concerns the Seminar has not yet fully explored. For the moment, the question of gender and power issues sparked a discussion of the relationship between Divine and human names.

"I find it oppressive when people introduce the notion of God as Father through analogy of the human father," said another of the Christians. "Christians call God 'Father' because Jesus did so! Calling God Father points out that there is a sense of fatherhood at which all fathers fail."

"The Name of God also tells us who we are," one Christian asserted; but this is complicated by the fact that both complexity and differentiation are at play. "Naming God does not have a reciprocal quality," she cautioned: "To call God 'Father' is not to say that all fathers are God. To say that God is a rock is not to say that rocks are God." It is important to keep this asymmetry in mind, she stressed. Sometimes, a person who assumes this power, who speaks God's words or Names, assumes identification with God. However, she explained, tradition also says that "the uniqueness of God's identity displaces and relativizes all human claims to power. So there is a sense in which the uniqueness of the Divine Name can function to undercut abuses in the Name of God. Not that abuses don't happen! But in the Names of God there are resources—both theological and devotional—precisely to undercut abuses and misuses of power."

One scholar called attention to Amina Wadud and other Muslim feminists who have said that the tawhidic paradigm rules out the very possibility that anyone might assimilate their authority to God's authority. The uniqueness of God rules out anyone else claiming power.[1]

Discussion of power and gender turned eventually to the Divine Name "Almighty." As one Christian explained, "To talk about God as 'Almighty' is not about pushing people around. Rather, it is about God as being the one who is never left without a possibility. God is never stopped, cornered, overwhelmed." One scholar underscored the importance of differentiating between dominion and domination: "We are thinking about lordship. What does 'lordship' look like? Dominion is different from domination. Learning to hear or tell that is quite difficult." Relatedly, another scholar emphasized the need to distinguish between "power over" and "power to do something"—between power as domination and power as competence. "Our texts place a very strong emphasis on the second one," he noted. "And we should not forget that the greatest power we humans have over each other is the power of attraction. That is extremely powerful—and it is that with which most of our texts play: God has an enormous attraction, even in our deepest and saddest points of grief; God relates to us in our relating to God.

Plenitude versus Uniqueness in Naming God

In naming God, one Christian observed, we encounter tension between plenitude and uniqueness—tension between the wealth of the Divine Names and the uniqueness of God's proper name. On the one hand, he observed, "it seems that the wealth of the Divine Names points to the superabundance of God—God as pure plenitude." Evidence is present in the writings of the Christians Dionysius and John of Damascus as well as in that of Muslim scholars Ghazālī and Tilimsānī. "All make this point," he declared: "this superabundance is important." Acknowledgment of God as pure plenitude, this scholar suggested, leads in turn to acknowledgment that "everything that exists in creation has its archetype in the perfections of God."

On the other hand, because God is "the one who is beyond being," characteristics of being cannot apply to God in the way they apply to creatures. He clarified:

> If God's proper name is He-Who-Is, then the uniqueness must be defined in such a way that everything-that-is participates in God; but God participates in nothing! This "participation in nothing" is pointed out by using a proper Name of God, thereby establishing a categorical ontological difference between the source of all Being and all being that has been—because in some way it participates in that source. If God is "Being Itself" in this way . . . then we cannot understand God under any classification concept. God may not be spoken of in such a way that God suffers from the restrictions or delineations of our definitions, and God is absolute Presence!

How is God present to us? How is everything else present to God? If God is that unique kind of being, is God just a being that can be named? These questions, it was agreed, await further consideration.

The Naming of God in Devotional Texts

How does our ability to interact with Names of God change as we move from scriptural to devotional mode? What challenges appear when we engage with devotional texts or actually participate in devotions? As the discussion of devotional literature got under way, a Christian reported that a member of his group had stressed how important it is to consider the way God is worshipped. How do people experience and talk about God? When one colleague pointed to John Mbiti's list of African Names of God, calling it "fascinating," another brought up the African woman's perspective, exemplified by Ghanaian oral theologian Afua Kuma (1908–1987), who named God in her context.

On Knowing God's Names

One can call upon God's Names only if one knows them, another participant pointed out. "You can't remember something unless you have learned it," she asserted. If we are to be able to recall God's Names in certain situations, or to be able to use them in talking to others, they need to be part of our makeup, and that, she stressed, "is one of the results of the practice of repetition." Facilitation of such practice is the role of devotional literature.

"Repetition!" one scholar declared. "Music makes the Names vibrate!" Music, vibration, can step in and play a unique role when reason is about to say something. "In Sufism," said another participant, "reason withdraws to make room for emotion and the experience of the heart. Qur'anic recitation raises the question not only of the presence of God in us but also how we are present to God. Music or practices like *dhikr* help us to set ourselves on the path of completion."

Among the items for study were several Christian hymns. As one group looked carefully at the stanzas of each, a recurring question was: Who is the subject and who is the object? One Christian clarified: "Often hymns start with a strong human subject. However, throughout hymnody, there is a subject change, where God becomes the subject, gifting God's presence to humans, enveloping humans in God's presence." A change occurs, he asserted: "the human—who had been a subject and agent of an activity—now becomes the recipient of a gift."

Among the Christian hymns under study, none commanded more attention in small-group sessions than "St. Patrick's Breastplate." One Muslim called its first stanza "extraordinary." Several Muslims had highlighted its reference to "the strong Name of the Trinity" and its repetition of "I bind unto myself." Its imagery of putting on the armor of God is indeed robust and visceral, a Christian confirmed.

It was one thing to study hymns as written items; quite something else to listen to them—which many participants did. "The addition of singing was both tender and powerful—sometimes simultaneously," said one of the Muslims. "It caused me to reflect again on the misuse of power."

Close reading of examples of *dhikr* caused one participant to assert that "the repetition in Islamic devotional texts and practice is something we Christians admire. It seems not to be a practice of owning something by repeating it. Rather, it seems to be a practice of being disowned, of being abandoned as a subject of the one who repeats, of being drawn into a reality in which our calling on God is part of God's relationship to us."

The seminar's discussion of hymnody revealed a variety of attitudes toward music. "Human beings talk most of the time," asserted a Christian. "Talking is one thing; but being embraced by the reality of God in music is quite different." For example, he said, for Lutherans, it is through music that the Names of God make the most sense. "It's not just that everything has a voice (as Paul says in 1 Corinthians)," he stressed, "but also, everything has a sound." Theologically speaking, hymn-singing is the vehicle for engagement as an embodied being. Through hymn-singing, humans join in the praise of creation.

Pastoral Implications

Studying the naming of God in devotional texts raised questions about the pastoral implications of such literature. One group enjoyed a deep discussion of a story from Rumi's *Mathnawi* in which a person crying out to God was mocked by the Devil. "The Devil had been saying, 'Well, where is the response?'" their reporter explained. "Then we came to a beautiful line about grief being greater than the empire of the world—that grief is, in a sense, a messenger of God." The story is beautiful; but how could it be put to use pastorally? As one Muslim explained, "while I find that story very poignant, I'm not likely to say to someone, 'I'm sorry for your loss; but don't worry! Rumi has this fantastic story that teaches that grief is actually a good thing!' Doing that has a way of shutting down the authenticity of that person's experience. The effect would be the opposite of our intent." People who offer consolation or pastoral care must give careful thought to when it would be appropriate to recount such a story. This group's recommendation was that we "develop a literacy, a knowledge, a familiarity with these stories, so that we can recollect them." It is similar with the Divine Names, he pointed out. "The Names are always out there; we can build up our familiarity with them. Then, when these moments arrive, we are no longer in a discovery process; rather, we are involved in a remembrance, a recollection—which we can connect back to the idea of *dhikr*."

Virtues of a Virtual Circle

In Christian-Muslim relationship, a Muslim scholar noted, the dialogue between our monotheistic foundations is one of continuity and discontinuity. The Divine Names are places of shared meaning, places of exchange, places between integration and modification. "In our discussions, we became keenly aware of the connections between theory and practice," one of the Christians observed:

> We thought about how we learn, how we understand, how we use the Names of God. At each of those turns, we found ourselves looking at the way that theology draws on scripture, of course; but also, how theology draws *upon* philosophy, and *from* the experience of praying. In reverse, we also became aware that what we say in theology has direct implications for how we are going to read the text, for what we say in philosophy, and what we do in our spiritual practice, particularly around the Names.

Whether one has in mind the Tetragrammaton or "the strong Name of the Trinity" or Names found in the Qur'an, it is one thing to discuss "What do these Names mean?" It is quite another—and far more interesting, said one Muslim—to consider "What work do these Names do? And how do we actually use them?" A refrain during his group's conversations was that "theological exploration is limited. It serves as guidelines or boundaries for the believer." An experiential understanding of the Names is equally important.

God's Names must not be considered independently from the narrative of God's revelation, one Christian insisted. In fact, he explained, "the Names communicate in an important way the story of God's revelation of who he is and how he relates to us." Furthermore, he argued strongly, God's Names should not be taken literally:

> The Names are pointers; they are icons that convey something from God, but not the fullness of God. The Names are another way to affirm the truth of God. None of the individual Names communicates the reality of God completely. However, the multiple Names, taken together, completely communicate the reality of God: that God is incomprehensible

> mystery. We have, through history, perceived something of God, but not the fullness.

"The most enriching aspect of our discussion," one scholar insisted, "was when our own individual stories or issues or questions were brought to the fore by reading these texts, by looking at particular Names. This was true whenever people tried to share a bit about their past and how a passage we were studying related to it. It was also true when raising thornier questions." The experience of collegial close reading of texts was most profound, said one Muslim, when his group had the opportunity to hear how colleagues re-constructed or recollected those texts, and how those passages led individuals to reflect on their own life narrative.

And, of course, questions lingered. As one scholar put it, the texts chosen for study during this convening had been "remarkable in content." He felt he had learned much from them; but, he said, "I also have the sad impression that I have not understood enough of the wealth of these texts nor of fullness of the thoughts expressed by my colleagues." Thinking of the entirety of this week of discussion of naming God, rather than of any particular text, one Christian wondered how confident the Islamic and Christian traditions (and the traditions within them) are that the difference between *essence* and *attribute* in God can be known and understood. "Distinctions and relationships between concepts such as *essence* and *attribute* are drawn by philosophy from observation of the world," she noted. "Since God is *other*, how do we properly guard the radical difference between how such ideas work with regard to God and how they work in all other cases?"

The logistical issues that had enabled a virtual circle may have felt strangely complex. Yet throughout the week the conversation in cyberspace had been as rich as ever. That should not have been a surprise since the participants in the nineteenth convening of the Building Bridges Seminar had arrived online with a strong connection to each other already in place. "We thank God for the friendship that we share, and the respect that had grown among us, and the community that has been created," said Daniel Madigan as he adjourned the virtuous circle; "and we look forward to the work we can do together in the future."

Note

1. One scholar noted that a similar point emerged when the Building Bridges Seminar discussed slaves and masters during convenings in 2017, 2018, and 2019. See Lucinda Mosher and David Marshall, eds., *Power: Divine and Human: Christian and Muslim*

Perspectives (Washington, DC: Georgetown University Press, 2019); Lucinda Mosher, ed., *A World of Inequalities: Christian and Muslim Perspectives* (Washington, DC: Georgetown University Press, 2021); and Lucinda Mosher, ed., *Freedom: Christian and Muslim Perspectives* (Washington, DC: Georgetown University Press, 2021).

Subject Index

Note: A separate index follows for Scriptural Citations.

Scriptural Citation Index

Bible

Qurʾan

About the Editor

Lucinda Mosher is the director of the Master of Arts in Interreligious Studies and an affiliate of the Macdonald Center for the Study of Islam and Christian-Muslim Relations at Hartford International University for Religion and Peace. Concurrently, she is senior editor of the *Journal of Interreligious Studies*, founding president of NeighborFaith Consultancy, and rapporteur of the Building Bridges Seminar. The author of six books, in addition to numerous chapters and journal articles, she is the editor or coeditor of nearly twenty titles—among them *The Georgetown Companion to Interreligious Studies* (2022) and nine Building Bridges Seminar volumes.

Printed in the USA
CPSIA information can be obtained
at www.ICGtesting.com
LVHW041928130923
758008LV00018B/2